"This dynamic parish priest brings to the book the wit and wisdom he shares with his parishioners. With a rare combination of warmth, insight, and vitality, he brings to us his driving commitment to helping people live God's Word in today's world. The twenty-nine sermons use specific Gospel readings as a springboard for succinct and insightful comments on current topics and events. These homilies will serve well to both teach and delight."

Book World

"The qualifying adjective 'timely' is important because Father Bausch's subjects are up to date, his references to topical events are illustrative, and his use of material from plays, films and literature is engrossing....

"Preachers will not merely repeat the content of Father Bausch's book, but they certainly will find many hints to enliven their own discourses. Will non-preachers also find it useful? I think so—as spiritual reading and to illuminate some of the passages from Scripture that are read on Sundays."

Msgr. Charles Diviney
The Tablet

"In his homilies, Father Bausch adds a new twist or two to each reading and applies it to our lives. For example, commenting on John 6:66–67, 'After this, many of his disciples left him and stopped going after him. Then Jesus said to the Twelve—What about you, do you want to go away too?' Father Bausch advises us to use our imaginations. 'Picture Jesus walking in the front door of the church, standing up here in front and looking each one of us in the eye and asking, "Will you also go away and leave the church?" The answer is yours to give.'"

The New Freeman

Also by Father William J. Bausch

Storytelling: Imagination and Faith
   (paper, 232 pages)

Pilgrim Church: A Popular History of Catholic Christianity
   (paper, 480 pages, revised and updated 1989)

*Becoming a Man: Basic Information, Guidance, and Attitudes
on Sex for Boys*
   (paper, 324 pages)

A New Look at the Sacraments
   (paper, 306 pages)

*The Hands-On Parish: Reflections and Suggestions for
Fostering Community*
   (paper, 192 pages)

Ministry: Traditions, Tensions and Transitions
   (paper, 176 pages)

The Christian Parish: Whispers of the Risen Christ
   (paper, 232 pages)

Take Heart Father: A Hope-Filled Vision for Today's Priest
   (paper, 192 pages)

Coming in May 1991:

More Timely Homilies
   (paper, 176 pages)

William J. Bausch

TIMELY
HOMILIES

The Wit and Wisdom of
an Ordinary Pastor

TWENTY-THIRD PUBLICATIONS
Mystic, Connecticut
and
the columba press
Dublin, Ireland

Acknowledgments

The excerpt (p. 151) from *The Velveteen Rabbit* by Margery Williams is reprinted with the permission of Doubleday, a division of Bantam, Doubleday, and Dell Publishing Group, Inc.

Permission to reprint (p. 155) an excerpt from *Fiddler on the Roof* was granted by the author, Sheldon Harnick.

Second printing 1990

Twenty-Third Publications
185 Willow Street
P.O. Box 180
Mystic, CT 06355
(203) 536-2611

ISBN 0-89622-426-0
Library of Congress Catalog Card No. 89-52152

The Columba Press
93 The Rise, Mount Merrion
Blackrock, Co Dublin
Ireland

ISBN 0-948183-97-7

Preface

"Gracious heavens!" he cries out, leaping up and catching
hold of his hair. "What's this? Print!"
—Charles Dickens

That Dickensian exclamation may come to mind—it did to
mine—when one has the audacity to put into print one's homilies. The origin of these pages is this. For a long while, unbe-
known to me, a gracious parishioner named Dorothy Boese
had been surreptitiously sneaking into the sacristy of our
church and recording my homilies. In due time I found out but
did not, of course, discourage her. In due time, I forgot all
about it and was not conscious any longer of her activity. Jerry
DiSalvo took over when Dorothy died.

Meanwhile the tapes were being quite widely passed
around, and those who were finding them helpful began to insist that they be put into print. I found myself not only generally reluctant to do such a thing, for there is a certain embarrassment involved, a certain sensitivity to being self-serving, but,
as a practical matter, did not think there would be a market for
them. Further encouragement—which I was only too happy to
receive—from my publisher tipped the scale. But the rationale
for this book remains. The hope that what has been preached
will help others on their spiritual pilgrimage.

Actually, all that I did was to pick out certain tapes and
have them transcribed, and that, for the most part, is what you
will find in these pages. Some slight editorial changes have
been made. Scripture references have been added in order to
make it easier for readers to follow the homilies. Bits of local
color and topical references can lend an air of immediacy to
the preached word, so almost all of these have been retained,

but with footnotes added for explanations where necessary. Here and there the clumsy syntax and phrases of the spoken word have been "cleaned up," but every effort has been made to retain the spontaneity of the homilies. I should also add that after Dorothy died, we were not able to locate all of the tapes of the homilies she recorded. What you have here, then, is the transcription of the best of the tapes we located. I do not save my notes for homilies, and even if I did it would make little difference—they are only one line notations, and after two weeks I can rarely make any sense of them.

There are a few matters regarding the texts of the homilies that should be discussed here. First of all, you will notice in these homilies the frequent use of the word "building" where others might ordinarily use the word "church." I have gotten into the habit of mostly speaking of the people as church, and they happen to meet and worship in this building and I take note of that distinction. Secondly, I realize that I am preaching to an educated—I almost said audience—congregation. But audience would not be amiss, for during homilies they are indeed hearers of the word. Accordingly my usual sources are the *New York Times*, entertainment, the arts, politics, the Scripture, and homily helpers in that order. I try to relate the Scripture to daily life, to everyday times, to local, national, and global happenings that impinge on our lives. Usually a current news item that is on everyone's mind is a jumping off point for preaching. I try to give the ancient readings a different twist, a new slant that relates to today. As a pastor I try to be sensitive to where the people are, where they're going, where they're leading me. Finally, some of these homilies tend to be longer than normal. "Normal," I am told, should be about five minutes. Alas, the homilies often run from ten to fifteen minutes. The only defense I can give is that no one seems to mind.

I know of no secret of a good homily, and readers will have to judge goodness or badness for themselves. For some, I would recommend that you read the text out loud, for, as you know, the sound of your voice delivering the word is different from silent reading. Reading aloud, indeed as if you yourself were proclaiming the homily, lends some passion, body movement, and involvement and gets a bit closer to the actual event. For others who might in fact be preachers, I suggest that you engage the imagination and picture yourself in the pulpit and in that conscious or unconscious living context that that privileged place evokes: facial expressions, staring down crying babies (fruitless), the gesture, the weather, the number and intensity of the coughs, the receptivity (or not) of the congregation, the stamina of the acolyte who may or may not faint in the middle of your best sentence, the sometimes sense of really being one with the congregation, the eccentricities of the microphone—and your own spirits and confidence (or lack thereof)—all provoke different nuances, so much so that drama can carry the day, a good anecdote and laughter can make the mediocre memorable, or just not being "on" can make the memorable forgettable. It's the difference, I suppose, between the live event and the recording. Finally, of course, for still others, a quiet reflective reading of these homilies might be just the thing.

Emily Dickinson wrote:

A word is dead
When it is said,
Some say.
I say it just
Begins to live
That day.

It is my prayer that these homilies, for all of you, will be words that begin to live.

I want to thank Gloria Ziemieski, who transcribed the tapes, Pat Kluepfel and Stephen Scharper from Twenty-Third Publications, who gave encouragement, and, most of all, the people. Not an anonymous mass but a beloved family, friends and fellow pilgrims.

To the "Morning Group"
Amicus est tanquam alter idem.

–Cicero

Contents

1

✛

Prayer

Luke 11:1–13

The Scriptures, of course, demand that we talk about prayer, since all of them are about prayer. And yet that is always hard to do, because in a way, it presupposes some expertise. And I suspect I have as many good times and bad times and difficulties with prayer as you do. But perhaps I could share some random remarks about prayer.

One is introduced by one of Eugene O'Neill's plays, *The Great God Brown,* and some of you may remember that toward the end the man is on his deathbed, and he's very frightened. And at his side is a woman who has become something of a mother-figure to him in these last moments of his life. And so she speaks to him as though he were a child, saying, "Go to sleep, Billy. It's all right." And he says, "Yes, mother." And then he starts to explain what he has experienced in life.

"It was dark," he says, "and I couldn't see where I was going, and they all picked on me." The woman then says, "I know. But you're tired now. Go to sleep." And he answers,

"And when I wake up?" She replies, "The sun will be rising."
Then Billy interrupts and says, in great seriousness, "To judge
the living and the dead." And in great fear, he adds, "I don't
want justice, I want love." And the woman replies quietly,
"There is only love." And as he dies, Billy begins to repeat the
words of the only prayer he knows: "Our Father who art in
heaven...."

Maybe my first remark is what Billy says. "I don't want justice," he says, "I want love." Most people pray. Statistically, all
the polls say that most people in the United States do pray,
and pray frequently. But what Billy shows us is that prayer
originates in our concept of God, and that's our first reflection.

St. John writes that "God is love." Billy fears that God may
just be justice. These are very different viewpoints, and your
viewpoint is going to color the way that you pray, if you pray
at all. Whether you see God as the all-seeing, critical eye, as
some of the art work has shown, or whether you see God as a
pair of arms that embraces you, obviously is going to influence
the way you're going to pray.

So in prayer you ask the first question: "What is my image
of God?" If for you God is a loving "Abba" and if you tend to
recall Jesus saying that when you address God say, "Our Father," prayer will likely come easier. If you envision God as a
strict taskmaster, filled with vengeance, prayer is going to become difficult. So if you have difficulty with prayer, what you
might look at first is what is your image of God, the one you
are praying to? What's that God like? A friend? Is God Abba?
Is God a lover? As the woman says, "Billy, there *is* only love in
heaven." That will encourage a great deal of prayer.

Secondly, most people pray in spurts. They don't always
pray morning and evening prayers, although some do. They
pray as the need arises, or when the Spirit moves them, or
when times are difficult.

There's a woman named Sandra Johnson who writes in
Commonweal magazine about her prayer life. She's married, the
mother of two girls; she also happens to be a lawyer; and besides, she teaches and lectures, and that puts her on the road

quite a bit. And with all of this, she has to make time for her family, her personal life, and for prayer. And she does. She is a woman who is trying to come to terms with all this, and she writes: "My husband and I belong to a prayer group with four other couples. We meet monthly, and have for the past six years or so. I also have been taking a three-day Passion Week retreat for each of the past five years, and a shorter retreat in Advent. I often guide my actions with a prayer. For example, I'm a lector at our parish, and each time I read I pray to the Holy Spirit that God will speak using my voice, and that the congregation will hear the word. Before I begin class I pray the prayer of Thomas Aquinas, asking for charm, wit, and wisdom in my teaching."

So there's a woman who has an enormously busy schedule, and yet she finds time for prayer. And still on the other side, she admits to a down side. She writes further (and I think we would resonate with this): "There are months when I don't pray. My prayer life is dry and my relationship with God is distant in those times. I will pray only at Sunday Mass, if then. Or make a quick sign of the cross more out of superstition than prayer."

She says this happens often when she gets involved in a project, or gets overly busy, and has a sense that she has no time for prayer.

"Well," you say, "that's a woman who's kinda got it all together." But there's also another side to her life that she'd like to share with you. She writes: "My husband, Bob, has multiple sclerosis. We've known for over five years, yet only recently have I been willing to listen to what that means in relationship to God's plan for me, as well as for him, and for our family as a whole." And she says she's able to cope with her husband's multiple sclerosis only with the help of her prayer group and reading the Scripture, and listening to their advice and their insights about prayer.

You see, there's the rub. And I like what she says. She's saying, "My husband, in the midst of good health, all of a sudden is stricken with MS, and I've got two children to raise, and we've got to do something before he gets so crippled we can't travel any more." But the question that she asks is, "What does this mean—this terrible tragedy—in relationship to God's plan for me?" And you see, the only way she can come to terms with that is through prayer, and I suspect it's the same for you.

What does it mean, you're being disappointed? What does it mean, you're being fired from your job? What does it mean to be alienated from members of your family? What does it mean to be divorced? What does it mean to be told of this terrible sickness you have to carry? What does it mean to come to terms with the decision to put mommy or daddy in a nursing home? What does all this terribleness mean? My child's on dope? Or my children are divorcing? Or my family's breaking up? Or whatever tragedy that we can go through, you and I?

And the only way you come to terms with that is in prayer. You want to know what this terrible tragedy means in reference to your relationship to God and the people involved. That's why we encourage you to get together with people, like-minded people, for Bible reading and for sharing. It helps a great deal to get insight and to get a view that you might not get by yourself.

There are two final things about prayer. One is what we call the prayer of embarrassment, and the other is the prayer of hindsight.

The prayer of embarrassment is for those people who suddenly run into difficulty. I hear this now and again. People start coming back to church because there's a terrible sickness. People suddenly start to pray because now they need God because they're in the ditch and they're suffering. They feel very embarrassed by that and they say, "I never go to church, and I never pray, and I never really think of God. Now that the chips are down, and now that the doctor told me I have cancer, all of a sudden I'm starting to pray, and I feel squeamish and guilty and embarrassed about that."

And to that declaration you or I might have the understandable reaction of saying: "Forget it. The only reason you're coming to us, and to God, and to the church now is because you have no place else to turn. Thanks a lot. We were here with you all the time and you didn't even look our way. Now suddenly that you've lost everything, you're knocking on our door for a loan. Buzz off!" That's likely to be our reaction.

But it is good to remember that the prayer of embarrassment is a valid prayer. You're dealing with God who has no pride. You're dealing with a God who is so humble and so foolish, and so stupid in our eyes, that this God runs to the prodigal son. This God sweeps the house looking for a penny, and leaves ninety-nine sheep to gather in the one.

God is probably the only one in our lives who stoops to conquer. So don't let that prayer of embarrassment ever put you off—or any of your friends. For us, it's unacceptable. For God, it's music to the ears and a joy to the heart.

The final remark has to do with what I call the prayer of hindsight. The prayer of hindsight relates to this fact: everyone who is over twenty-five knows that as you go through life there are things that you're going through that are terrible and horrible and indeed they are, and they leave scars. But if you live long enough, you also look back in hindsight and say, "I'd never like to go through that again, but there was, in fact, a grace there." When you were left back in school and didn't graduate from high school, it was horrible to go through. But in hindsight you see great grace, what God has done for you.

Or maybe you had a terrible disease and were not supposed to live beyond seven years old. You were anointed as an infant. In those days, it meant certain death. In hindsight, you see what it's done for your sympathy for the sick and the poor, what God has done that way.

So when you look in hindsight, there are often the hidden graces—in death, in disappointment, in fracture, in hurt, in pain and suffering, and in loss. Our greatest saints have come through adversity precisely as saints.

They found on a Confederate soldier in the Civil War this little prayer which has become known as the "Confederate Soldier's Prayer." I'd like to call it, "The Hindsight Prayer." You

may have heard it before, but I'd like to share it with you, and
end with it:

I asked God for strength, that I might achieve;
I was made weak, that I might learn humbly to obey.
I asked for health, that I might do greater things;
I was given infirmity, that I might do better things.
I asked for riches, that I might be happy;
I was given poverty, that I might be wise.
I asked for power, that I might have the praise of men;
I was given weakness, that I might feel the need for God.
I asked for all things, that I might enjoy life;
I was given life, that I might enjoy all things.
I got nothing that I asked for,
But everything I had hoped for.
Almost, despite myself, my unspoken prayers were an-
    swered.
I am, among all men, truly blessed.

2

+

The Body of Christ

Matthew 26:17–30

Today is a day in the Memorial Day weekend, of course, and at long last, a glorious one at that, hardly a time, in a way, to give a heavy message. And yet I ask you to bear with me with this reflection because, coincidentally, Memorial Day and the feast we're celebrating, the Body of Christ, have something deeply in common. [The feast of Corpus Christi falling on the Memorial Day weekend. Memorial Day, celebrated late in May, commemorates all United States war dead.]

Let me start off with something I picked out of the paper the other day. It was a speech that Father Byron, the Jesuit who's the president of Catholic University, gave at a commencement exercise. The title of this speech was "Why Kids Do Drugs and the Culture That Abhors Pain." He comments:

Deep down on the demand side of the problem of drug abuse in America lie three causal considerations. First, a desire, known to every normal, healthy person, to experience the exhilaration of a high. The second causal consideration of the demand side for drugs is the desire to avoid pain, physical or psychological pain. In a culture that cannot tolerate the thought of pain, physical or psychological, it isn't surprising that avoidance of all pain, at

all times, by all means, would become something of su-
preme value. Third, our cultural denigration of pain, disappointment, discouragement, and monotony, encourages
escape at any cost.

There are also reasons why normal young people want
to avoid pain. Most are obvious. Less obvious is the fact
that commercial advertisements have instructed them to
take pills for the elimination of headache and heartburn
long before they know what these maladies mean. Pain
has no redemptive value in the value system of a secular
society.

I think that's what I want to focus in on with you if you stick
with me on this. Pain has no redemptive value in a secular society like our own, which means, when you come down to it, it
has no meaning. It has no meaning in an instant world. In a
world where each person is viewed as a separate atom and a
solitary individual.

We are taught almost daily that we are free-floating organ-
isms, a bundle of selfish genes; that we are unrelated and un-
connected to others. Well, in this scenario, of course, pain becomes utterly without meaning and utterly ridiculous. And so
hurts and deficiencies must be regulated by drugs. Are you
sad? Crack will give you a high. Are you weak? Steroids will
give you muscles. Are you anxious? Tranquilizers will help
you face moody customers at the airport counter.

But in the old days, we had something else to do with pain
and suffering. We could offer it up for the souls in purgatory,
and anyone else, for that matter. And I ask you, what teacher
or what parent here has said in the last five years to your children, "Offer it up for the souls in purgatory"?

It's such a quaint thought. It provokes ridicule and smiles, as
we might remember, those of us who are thirty-five and older,
the arithmetic games of running in and out of church on Holy
Thursday, computerizing indulgences for the poor souls. You
do remember? Or you might remember visions of unbalanced
saints, beating themselves, all rather barbaric and unhealthy.

And we've outgrown that. So there's no doubt about it, offering up sufferings for others does quite boggle the modern, individualistic mind.

And yet I would say this, If you dig deep enough, beneath the nonsense, and the exaggeration, and the weird, you'll find an enormous Christian truth. Simply, it is this: We are the body of Christ and we are connected. The Christian witness says that we are in physical, psychical, spiritual relationship with one another. We can plead for one another, we can pray for one another. We can offer up acts of courage, endurance, and sufferings for others. Why, we can even die, and somehow in the great mystery of life and love, it can benefit others.

It is not just that Sidney Carton took the place of his friend on the gallows in Dickens's *Tale of Two Cities*. It's not just that St. Maximilian Kolbe took the place of a prisoner in a concentration camp and died in his stead. It's not just that innumerable United States' soldiers in World War I and II, and in the Korean and Viet Nam wars, and in all the other wars, died for us that "we might be free." What's important for us to remember today is that human beings can do these things because we are spiritually joined; because we are spiritually united we can direct our energies, and our prayers, and our sufferings on behalf of other people for their welfare.

We can see in suffering a kind of intensified love for others. We can lay down our lives, we can endure hardships, to energize grace for another. We can jump boundaries, psychically and spiritually. After all, if our cleanliness or our pollution affects other people on the other side of the globe, if our decisions can influence the decisions of others, if our moods can modify others' behavior, why not our prayers? And our pain? And our sufferings, for the souls in purgatory, or anybody else?

The Christian believes in spiritual ecology, if you will. So we ask ourselves, is our Memorial Day just chalking up a mental image of those who died for our freedom, or can we really pray for them? Is it absurd that if you have asthma, let us say, that you can offer some of your discomfort of your asthma for those who are suffocating in New York tenements on a hot summer's day?

Is it silly for you, lying on your hospital bed, to offer your pain for those who are languishing in nursing homes? Is it ridiculous for you, when you are hungry, to offer up some of your hunger for those who daily go to sleep without anything to eat? Is it outrageous for you to offer up your migraine headache, your pain, your cancer, your sickness, for hardened sinners? And for those you love?

A society that sells immortality, face-lifts, cosmetic corpses, and pills for every occasion, says, "Yes, it is absurd. Suffering has no meaning." Or as Father Byron puts it, "It has no redemptive value." And that leaves our children with nothing to do with pain and discomfort and boredom, except to turn to drugs for relief, to get their high.

But to find meaning and purpose and dignity in human suffering gives us that sense of solidarity. It's a happy coincidence, I think, that Memorial Day happens to fall on the Feast of the Body of Christ because they come together to remind us that remembrance and intercession go together. And that offering pain and disappointment, and even life itself, for another, reveals a deep mystery about ourselves. That we have solidarity. That we can teach our children to offer up suffering rather than to reach for a pill. And that there might be some merit in the Christian scheme of things.

So I guess, basically, it comes down to this: For those of us who are believers, and those of us who are gathering in worship here—do you believe, on the gut level, that we are interrelated? Do you believe that through baptism we have become the mystical body of Christ? Do you believe, as you will say in the creed in a few minutes, in the communion of saints?

Do you believe in the power of the soldiers who died for us, to set us free? Do you believe in Jesus, who died on the cross, so that we might live forever? Do you believe that you can influence others? Affect others? Do you believe that powerful mystery that we can offer up much for others and touch their lives? You see, these are the questions that make us ponder as Memorial Day happily falls on the same day as the Feast of the Body of Christ.

Again, I suspect that teachers and parents today don't say much about this kind of interrelatedness of solidarity because it's such a difficulty for our modern minds. But reflect for a minute. It's been proven that people can physically influence one another across the miles. People have the powers of clairvoyance. People have powers of telepathy. Why is it absurd to think that my aching tooth, my sickness, my discomfort, my boredom, can be offered up, and in some unknown, mysterious way touch those who are profoundly my brothers and sisters?

Why are we reluctant, with our modern minds, to teach this to our children? To help them to realize that as life goes along, there are ups and downs, and there are pain and sorrow. All this just goes with the human condition. Nobody escapes it here, you or I. But isn't it also nice to know, in the Christian tradition, that there can be meaning to something which basically is absurd? That by the grace of God, suffering can be redemptive, and that in an unknown way, we can gain graces for countless others?

It is only when you believe that you're an atom that you find it silly. It is only when you believe in the body of Christ; it is only when you and I break this bread and share this cup, and call one another brother and sister; it is only when we make the gesture as a sign of peace; it is only when the ups and downs and our lives and deaths resonate with each other that we can say, "There is something here." And to offer it up is not just a silly Christian platitude; it's profound and it's mystery.

And God only knows, and I guess we'll only know someday, that many of the graces that we have gained, and many of the good things that have happened to us, have been because some unknown lover has offered it up for those who needed it most. It happened to be you and me, at the moment.

Who wants pain? Nobody. But it comes. Who wants to be bored? Nobody. But it happens. Who wants to be sick? Nobody. But there it is. Who wants to say that it's utterly useless and meaningless? Only those without faith. Who wants to say, "Offer it up for others"? Those living the Christian experience.

3

Choose

John 6:66–67; Joshua 24:14–15

I'm too seasoned to try to talk about that second reading,* but I would like to talk about the first and the third. And in the first and the third readings, there is a similar motif. The motif is one of choosing.

You recollect that Joshua said to the people, "Look, choose. Will you serve the true God, or go after false Gods?" In the gospel Jesus gives a similar challenge. He says, "Look, choose. Do you also wish to leave me?" You have your choice. Choose one or the other.

When you think about it, in the Catholic church, people are seldom, I think, given that kind of a dramatic choice. This is probably mostly because we don't have any criteria for membership, when you come down to it. So, very few people are confronted that way. I think what happens in the Catholic church is that people just very quietly decide, for one reason or another, to leave on their own. And I dare say that there's probably nobody in this building right now who hasn't had some neighbor or relative or friend or family member who has left the Catholic church, for whatever reasons. Nothing big, nothing dramatic, they just faded out for whatever reasons in their own hearts.

*Ephesians 5:24—"Let wives be subject to their husbands in all things."

But the other side of the question is the intriguing one, I
think, today, and it refers to you and me. And it is this question: why do you stay? Why are you here this morning, and
every weekend? Is it just habit? Fear of sin? Punishment? Part
of your ethnic background or whatever? That's the question:
not, will you go away? but, why do you stay?

All of you are familiar, of course, with Father Andy Greeley,
for many reasons. Awhile ago he had an article in *America*
magazine, and he was addressing precisely this question: Why
do Catholics stay? And with one little caveat, he said his research has shown that Catholics stay in the Catholic church for
two reasons. One, because of their heritage, both their ethnic
and their religious heritage; and secondly, because of the eucharist. They are drawn by what you and I are drawn by in the
breaking of the bread, the presence of Jesus in this great sacrament.

The caveat that he gave was this—he said that people stay
for heritage and eucharistic reasons in spite of indifferent, or
backward, or bad clergy. So one of my peers wrote a letter to
the editor, and rightly so, and he said, "Well, if you listen to
Greeley talk, it seems that all the priests in the country have
some kind of huge computer network, and we all get together
and find out how we can give wretched homilies and put the
people down. No, we try like everybody else, and we run the
gamut like everybody else." But it still comes back to the question, regardless of the goodness or badness or indifference of
your priests or leaders or whoever, you have to come back to
your own question: Why do you stay? or, Why are you here
this morning?

And I think that the answer to these questions basically
comes down to this. That people have enough perception to realize that what draws them here is a relationship with Jesus. It
is not a profound or fundamental relationship with either the
pope, or the bishop, or the pastor; it is a relationship with
Christ. And somehow, in our instincts, we realize that for two
thousand years, for all of its ups and downs, the church mediates *that* Jesus Christ.

Sometimes people say, "I don't need a church to be religious," but that's somewhat like saying, "I don't need a school to be educated." And that's true—I suppose you could get educated without school, but generally, if the school does its job, it mediates a lot of learning or ways to learn and to grow. And the same way with the church. We need the church, because for all of its flaws and faults, it mediates that instinct and experience that we have for Jesus Christ. It gives us meaning, helps us to get a handle on life.

I'm reading Tom Clancy's *The Hunt for Red October*, you know, one of the great spy novels that Tom writes. *The Red October*, as some of you who've read it know, is the name of a Soviet sub-ship, a super sub-ship. The captain, Marco Remius, is defecting from the Soviet Union because he's a Lithuanian who has seen the brutality of the Soviets who came in and took over his country, and also suppressed the Roman Catholic church in that country. And so he's gone through the ranks, and finally he's going to steal the Soviet sub, and through the whole book he has the Soviet navy looking for him; and the Americans and the English—kind of very exciting.

But early on, one of the passages in the book describes his inner thoughts, particularly concerning his wife, Natalja, who died because of the bungling of the Soviet medical system. This little paragraph is there: "Marco Remius watched the coffin of his wife roll into the cremation chamber to the solemn strain of a classical requiem, wishing that he could pray for Natalja's soul, hoping that Grandmother Hilda, who had had him secretly baptized as an infant, had been right. That there was something beyond the steel door and the mass of flame. Only then did the full weight of the events strike him. The state had robbed him of more than his wife—it had robbed him of a means to assuage his grief with prayer. It had robbed him of hope, if only an illusion, of ever seeing her again."

I think that's part of it. That you and I have those basic instincts that say that life does have ultimate meaning in spite of its absurdity, and this church of ours does, in fact, mediate an answer, an eternal life.

Another person who wrote a letter to the editor of *America* magazine, a woman named Judy Drake, said, "Look, we stay Catholics because we not only accept the clergy on its very human terms, but because we can now welcome the inclusion of clergy as members of the body of Christ, standing next to us instead of above us. Anyway, try as they might, there is nothing the Vatican, the priests, or the bishops can do to drive us out of the church. We will continue to stay because we seek to imitate Our Lord, not any member of the clergy." And again, you see, her answer—which, I think, is probably an authentic answer for all of us—that somehow we perceive and seek the Lord. That Jesus is the reason, ultimately, if we press it hard enough, as to why we're here.

It brings to mind an old quotation from Frank Sheed, that lovely layman of another era. In his wisdom and experience as husband and father and Catholic, he wrote these words, and they're worth repeating:

> We are not baptized into the hierarchy; do not receive the cardinals sacramentally; will not spend an eternity in the beatific vision of the pope. St. John Fisher could say in a public sermon, "If the pope will not reform the curia, God will." A couple of years later he laid his head on Henry VIII's block for papal supremacy followed to the same block by Thomas More, who had spent his youth under the Borgia pope, Alexander VI, lived his early manhood under the Medici pope, Leo X, and died for papal supremacy under Clement VII, as time-serving a pope as Rome ever had.
>
> *Christ* is the point. I, myself, admire the present pope, but even if I criticized him as harshly as some do, even if his successor proved to be as bad as some of those who have gone before, even if I sometimes find the church as I have to live in it, a pain in the neck, I should still say that nothing a pope could do or say would make me wish to leave the church, although I might well wish that *he* would leave.

Israel, through its best periods, as through its worst, preserved the truth of God's oneness in a world swarming with gods, and a sense of God's majesty in a world sick with its own pride. So with the church. Under the worst administration we could still learn Christ's truth, receive his life in the sacraments, be in union with him to the limit of our willingness. In awareness of Christ, I can know the church as his mystical body, and we must not make our judgment by the neck's sensitivity to pain.

I think that's basically it. No matter what we discover, or what our experience has been, no matter what the reasons our friends and family members give for leaving the church, I think that challenge of today's Scripture comes back to us— that question that Jesus asks: "Will you also go away?" And I think that basically we say "no" because we realize, in Peter's words, "You have the words of eternal life." That in spite of all the movies, like *The Last Temptation of Christ,** the fact is that we perceive Jesus as the victor over death. We also understand that he's not just a great philosopher, or a good person, but there's something more. Ultimately we share Peter's conviction: "You are the Holy One." And in this two-thousand-year tradition that we're in, we are still listening to this word of Scripture, the same one for two thousand years, and in a few minutes we shall celebrate a eucharist that Peter and Paul celebrated; and break bread and know the presence of Christ in our fractured lives.

So there's a question that the Scriptures pose for us today; and maybe in your mind's eye you can use your imagination and just picture Jesus walking in the front door of the church and standing up here in front of these flowers, and turning around and looking each one of us in the eye, and asking, "Will you also go away?"

And the answer? That's yours to give.

---

*The movie focuses on the humanness of Jesus Christ, and particularly on sexual temptation.

4

✛

Forgiving – Being Forgiven

Matthew 18:21–35

There are two very powerful questions that today's readings raise, and of course, they center around forgiveness.

The first question is this: How does one forgive the unforgivable? That was the question raised by Simon Weisenthal's book, *The Sunflower*, for those of you who read it. The book is somewhat biographical, about an incident during the two years that Weisenthal spent in a Nazi concentration camp. Like so many others, his pain was extremely intense. Eighty-nine members of his family had died in these Nazi concentration camps. He had watched helplessly while his mother was shoved into one of those boxcars, never to be seen again, as she rode off to her death. With his very own eyes, he saw his mother-in-law machine-gunned right in front of him, so he had reason to have great pain.

He tells the story that one day when he was in the concentration camp, a nurse came out to where he was working, tapped him on the shoulder, and told him to follow her. And he is taken to a make-shift hospital, to a very small room. In that room there is a single bed. On this bed is a person who is almost completely wrapped in bandages, looking very much like a mummy. It is obvious that this person is soon to die. The nurse leaves him alone in the room with the bandaged body, and the dying person begins to speak. The bandaged body is that of a very young man, twenty-one years old, a member of the dreaded SS troops. The young man tells his story:

He had been raised a Catholic, but in his teens he had joined the Hitler youth. He had abandoned his Catholicism in favor of his new religion, which demanded all he could give—total obedience and reverence to a new god called Adolf Hitler. When the war broke out he volunteered immediately for the elite SS troops. He wanted to be a part of the easy and the quick victory that the Nazi propaganda had promised him. While he was in the eastern zone, he was given the assignment of dealing with the Jews in the local area. To deal with the Jews in the local area meant just one thing. And so his unit gathered up all the Jews and herded them into a building. They doused the building with gasoline, set up machine guns to take care of those who tried to escape, and they set it on fire, which was the common procedure.

This incident troubled this young SS trooper. Some of the Catholic teachings he had received while a child began to be stimulated. He began to be preoccupied with what he had done. In fact, his preoccupation led him to such distraction that he grew careless; and the result of his carelessness was that in a skirmish, he was riddled with bullets. And here he was, lying bandaged, in an isolated room in a make-shift hospital. One of the things that was on his mind was that above all, he wanted forgiveness. And so he had requested that a Jew would be sent in—any Jew. Male Jew, female Jew, a representative Jew—he wanted one of them there. And just by circumstance, the nurse had tapped Simon Weisenthal, who had gone into this room and listened to the story and heard this man's plea. This man, this young boy, said he was not born a murderer and he didn't want to die a murderer; and he begged Simon, on behalf of his people, for forgiveness. And Weisenthal says that the only response he could give was to get up and leave the room without saying a word, without granting forgiveness.

Later on, his non-response troubled him. Should he have granted forgiveness? But after all, my God! His own family, eighty-nine of them, had been destroyed; and this Nazi SS trooper had been a part of all kinds of horrible atrocities and murder and killing. He had committed all kinds of crimes. Was forgiveness possible? Should he grant it? And he concludes this story by asking the reader, you and me, to put ourselves in his shoes and ask ourselves the question: "What would I have done?" An interesting question, isn't it? What would you and I have done?

In the second part of the book he gives the replies of twenty-one of the people who answered the question. It was significant that of the twenty-one people, many of them were Christian, and without exception the Christians who responded cited Jesus' example and the hard, tough words of his gospel, such as we heard this morning. The revealing fact is that somehow, in spite of the dilemma and the hardship, they felt an imperative thrust that forgiveness should have been given. But still, if we were in his shoes, and were faced with someone representing a group that killed eighty-nine members of our family—put yourself in his shoes—could you have forgiven? That's the first question to contemplate—the first question the gospel throws in our faces.

But if the first question thrown out by the gospel is: Can we forgive others?, then I think maybe the second question is even more powerful and disturbing. But before getting to that question, I should interject that I fully realize that the suffering we endure isn't comparable to that endured by Simon Weisenthal, and yet his situation has great implications for us. That said, the second question I would share with you begins with a reversal of roles. In the first role I asked you to stand in Simon Weisenthal's shoes and ask yourself that question: Could you forgive? Now I ask you to reverse it and make believe you're the Nazi. What if others—what if the Simon Weisenthals in your life—cannot, will not, or are unable to forgive you? For example:

There's the parent who has been, and who is, an alcoholic;

who in his drinking days was abusive to his children, shamed and embarrassed them, poisoned their minds, turned their hearts and left them with great scars. His children by this time have left home. He has gone to AA and recovered, hasn't had a drink in years, but now his children, disgusted from years of abuse, want no part of him. Yet he, before he dies, is desperate for their forgiveness. They are either unwilling or unable to forgive. He's lying there in this pain. What does he do?

Or here's the wife who for many years and many affairs has betrayed her husband, and has now come to her senses, but has left a great distrust and a gap and a chasm of miscommunication and a deep and abiding hurt. The husband doesn't know if he can forgive. What does he do?

Or there's the boy who in his selfishness has exploited a girl, gotten her pregnant, and either has paid for or insisted upon an abortion so he'd have no responsibility; or he's got a boy or a girl, a son or daughter somewhere on this planet for whom he has not taken one iota of responsibility. And as the irresponsibility of his actions comes close to him, he wants to go and find his son or daughter and get down on his knees and say, "I'm sorry." But he doesn't even know who his child is.

Or there are brothers and sisters of the same family who say to me, "We haven't spoken to each other in twelve to fifteen years." They want forgiveness; and it's not forthcoming.

The second question is this: What about the people we've hurt? The people we've wounded who won't forgive, who can't forgive; or maybe they're dead already? It's like the man who calls me every three months. (You may have read about this years ago in the paper. He killed his wife and his two children, nine and eleven years old.) He calls me every three or four months asking, "Do you think they're in heaven? Do you think they were old enough to commit sin? Do you think they are in hell?" What he's asking me is not so much about their eternal salvation; what he's asking me is, "Can my dead children forgive me?" He is loaded with guilt.

What about the people who are dead and we cry over their graves? The guilt is heavy, very heavy. And we want forgiveness so badly, like that young Nazi, before we die; and the Simon Weisenthals of our lives have simply disappeared or they have turned their backs and they have walked away.

There are two reactions to this. Let me give you an extreme case in another vein. I remember twenty years ago a girl named Ellen. She was very, very pretty, as I found out later from her photograph; lovely, talented girl, and she did some work in a little theater in New York. One of the writers who used to write for the old *Saturday Evening Post* had connections. He saw her, liked her; she was on the way to becoming a professional. He had friends in Los Angeles; he arranged for her to go for an interview. She bought a new wardrobe; she was excited. This was the beginning of a glorious career. She said goodbye to her family; she stooped down to say goodbye to her pet dog. In his frolicking, he reached up and scratched her a little bit on the cheek, but it didn't matter because a little makeup would cover that.

She went to Los Angeles, and as sometimes happens, her luggage got lost. She was unnerved at that. The man who was supposed to meet her was late, and she was really getting unstrung; she was getting nervous. Finally he came, but she had gotten so upset and nervous that she began to cry; and on top of that the scratch on her cheek was infected. So between the crying and the infection and not having a wardrobe, she was in no mood to see anybody; she was a mess. They were very kind to her. They said, "Go home, get yourself together, and come back."

She went home and she retreated. She would see nobody. She began to eat too much and got very heavy. This alarmed her because her father died from obesity; so she went to the other reaction; she went on a starvation diet. When I met her she was like skin stretched over bone. I talked to her and her mother. (Her mother, who was a widow, had doted on the daughter.) I suggested that she was at a point where she needed psychiatric care. They were very offended at that. Finally, she went to a psychiatrist I knew, and he said he couldn't do anything for her; just suggested getting her some vitamins and trying to build her up. She died. She died of starvation, with plenty of food on the table. And her mother said she died talking of the interview that went wrong, like it happened last week instead of twenty years ago.

That's the first reaction we can take to our guilt: Turn into ourselves and destroy ourselves. Or else we can turn to Jesus, and when we have the Simon Weisenthals who will not and cannot forgive us, this is the Jesus that comes in and takes on their identity, and steps into the place of those we have hurt so badly they can't forgive us. And Jesus steps into the shoes of the Simon Weisenthals and he comes to our bandaged and broken bodies and hearts and he hugs us and he kisses us and he says, "All is forgiven." And he loves us. When people won't forgive, Jesus will. When people can't forgive, Jesus will. When people are unable to forgive, Jesus will, because this is the other part of the gospel.

This is the gospel that says the shepherd left ninety-nine sheep to look for the one. This is the gospel that says the woman left nine coins to look for one. Above all, it's the gospel of the prodigal son—when the son repented, the father went to meet him, and showered him with kisses. So the gospel's powerful. It tells us of two ways, and there are two questions it imposes. If you are Simon Weisenthal, the gospel challenges you with the imperative, the demand, to forgive. And if you are the young Nazi, and you so badly want forgiveness, and the people of your life can't or won't, or are unable to forgive, then you turn to the gospel and you find out that Jesus Christ will stand in their place.

This is also, I suggest, why he invented the sacrament of confession, or reconciliation. Maybe some of you have shied away from that sacrament, but believe me, it's the place Jesus has set up where you and I are reconciled to the Father; it's the one place where we can be reassured that in our broken and dying moments the Lord Jesus will come and say, "Go in peace, your sins are forgiven. I, on behalf of your mother, your brother, your daughter—all those people who will not forgive—I will forgive." And it is this sacrament that makes those moments glorious. So the Scripture, my friends, is powerful; and it leaves us with those two questions to ponder today. Am I Simon Weisenthal? Before I die, I'd better come to terms with the gospel. Am I the young Nazi? Before I die, I must come to terms with the Lord Jesus.

5

The Transfiguration: The Lesson

Luke 9:28–36

I find this gospel account of the transfiguration to be exceedingly intriguing because when you analyze it, it's basically a story not only of life, but of invitation.

You take the elements of the story, which we know so well. There is the transfiguration—the sudden vision, the great glory. All of us have those moments. There's the wedding day. There's the first job. There's the adventure. There's the first home, the first child. And all of these things are there in their splendid form, and they shine forth with joy. Just try to remember all those visions that you have had.

Just try to remember—those of you who are married—your wedding day. Try to remember your first house that you bought. The first car. The first job. The first paycheck. And there is something transfigured, and life is fulfilled, and there it is, glorious. And the transfiguration story gives us that.

But secondly, it also introduces something else which we enter into very easily. Notice what Peter said. After he sees this marvelous vision, he says, "Well, let's build three booths here, one for you, one for Moses, and one for Elijah." In short what he's saying is: "This is so wonderful. Let's hold on to it forever. Let's freeze the moment." And if you think that's a far-off story of two thousand years ago, you're wrong—this is our story every day. Under the pressure of the media and advertisers, we're always asked to freeze the moment. We're always asked to say "and they lived happily ever after." We're always asked to look at the gorgeous apartments and clothes and lifestyles and say "this is the way it is forever," and advertising encourages that.

But of course realism comes along and says "that's impossible." Even with the most wonderful dream house, sooner or later you have to clean the gutters. Even the most ardent kiss, sooner or later you gotta to come up for air. Even the most fervent handshake, sooner or later gets sweaty. Even the most perfect wedding day, sooner or later, there's conflict because you're two people, and not really one, yet.

And so Peter, of course, represents the foolishness. He represents the escapism, if you will. He represents modern advertising. "Freeze the moment. Let's build three booths. This is it forever. Let's hold on to it."

And then the third element comes in, which is interesting. Enter the scenario two spoilsports, by the names of Moses and Elijah. And while Peter is rhapsodizing about this moment because he's just gotten his first car or his first house, Moses and Elijah are whispering to Jesus. And what are they whispering about? Well, they tell us. They are whispering to Jesus about his passage to Jerusalem, which is the translation for his passion, his suffering, and his death. Here they come along and mess up the whole picture. There's Jesus in his magnificent, splendiferous glory, all ablaze and light and white, and these two come along and talk about his passage and his suffering.

But when you take that whole story, what Luke is saying is, "This is not only the Christian life, this is the story of every human journey. And every human journey unfolds in basically five steps after the transfiguration."

The first step is always the revision of the dream. As I said before, reality sets in. Your feelings toward each other on the wedding day and ten years later are not quite the same, are they? They may be better, hopefully. They may be worse. But they're not the same. The realities of biology come in. People do get sick. Children do throw up, and diapers have to be changed. And death intrudes. Death and sickness. And all of a sudden, you see, we begin to revise the dream. We don't want it in its present form. We'd like to build those three booths and hold on to it at its best forever, but Moses and Elijah are turning out to be correct after all. There's some kind of passage, some kind of passion or suffering or change, that's demanded. And you almost get the full sense of the story—some change is going to be demanded in order to recapture the original ideal. And so you begin to revise the dream somewhat.

The second stage of the journey is, of course (it hits all of us), the temptation to escape because, in fact, the transfiguration did not freeze forever, like the advertisers promised. And usually the escapism takes two forms. It takes the form of cynicism. So we make all those marriage jokes, and we make all those husband and wife jokes, and the job jokes, and things like that, covering up our cynicism that arises because the promise didn't hold up. The job after a while got boring. The house got too small. We needed a better neighborhood. The friendship soured or was betrayed. Our darling children turned out to disappoint us. And we begin to have a sense of the loss of expectation and the loss of the wonderful. It's in this stage, by the way, where most divorces take place.

That reminds me of the story of the man who walked into a talent agent's office to see if there were any openings for a specialty act. The agent said, "Well, what do you do?" And the man said, "I imitate birds." And agent said, "Hey, I can't use you. Bird imitations are a dime a dozen. You're just wasting my time. Get the heck outta here!" Whereupon the man flapped his arms and flew out the window. You see, it's that kind of thing. The cynicism, the loss of expectation of any kind of wonderful occurrence.

Or the other form it takes is that you begin to overlay the original vision and ideal with pragmatism. You begin to turn what started out as poetry into prose. You begin to deal with your friendships and your marriages in terms of legalisms and rights, and the message gets lost.

Some clever person did a little parody of one of the gospels, and I would like to share it with you:

Then Jesus took his disciples up on the mountains, and when they had gathered around him, he taught them, saying, "Blessed are the poor in spirit, theirs is the kingdom of heaven. Blessed are those who mourn. Blessed are those who hunger and thirst for righteousness. Blessed are the merciful, the pure of heart. Blessed the peacemakers. Blessed are those who are persecuted for righteousness' sake, for theirs is the kingdom of heaven."

Then Simon Peter said, "Are we supposed to know this?"

And Andrew said, "Do we have to write this down?"

And James said, "Will we get a test on this?"

And Philip said, "I don't have any paper."

And Bartholomew said, "Do we have to turn it in?"

And John said, "The other disciples don't have to learn this."

And Matthew said, "I have to go to the bathroom."

And Judas said, "What does this have to do with real life?"

And one of the Pharisees present asked to see Jesus' lesson plans, and inquired of Jesus, "What is your terminal objective? Have you completed a task analysis? What about a diagnostic survey?"

And Jesus wept.

We do that. That's the second stage, which occurs even though we thought we would hold on to the transfiguration forever, without movement.

The third stage of the journey, of course, begins a turnabout for those who persist. That's the time when you begin to take on and to share one another's burdens, both in sympathy and in wisdom, because, you see, you realize that life isn't the ideal that the television says, but has to be worked at. This stage usually requires a certain amount of reflection, a great deal of prayer, and sometimes it does require a trauma. There's a loss; there's a sickness; you lose your job. You're disappointed with your children. There's an addiction that you struggle with. But nevertheless, through this you begin to build empathy. You begin to see people in a different light because your weaknesses are apparent and you begin to accept their weaknesses. And that begins to be a movement.

Then you hit the fourth stage, which is really an advance. As you go through life, you begin to get to the level of acceptance on your life's journey. And you accept life—not in defeat, that's important—but you accept it in love. It's like Jesus who looked at the young man, and loved him. It's like Jesus who looked at Magdalene, and saw possibility. It's like Jesus, who saw Matthew, the tax collector, and said, "Come, follow me." It's when your vision begins to see people with the eyes of Christ.

And then, of course, you hit the fifth level. You get the ideal back. You get the transfiguration that you started out with, but now transformed. Not with all the splendor of Mount Tabor, not with all the razzle-dazzle of white robes, and voices, and clouds, but a true and sincere transfiguration of life and love that you never dreamed possible. These are the whole people. These are the people who now understand what Moses and Elijah were whispering about. It was necessary for Jesus to go through his terrible passage for his transfiguration, in glory, and it is the same for us.

There's a very marvelous writer, Madeleine L'Engle, who writes a lot of children's books. She's a prize-winner. One of her books is *Two-Part Invention*, the story of her forty-five year marriage to a cancer victim and actor, Hugh Franklin, who now is dead. And I'd like to quote one or two lines of hers. As she was sitting beside Hughie's bed and watching as he was dying, she wrote: "I am who I am because of our years together, freed by his acceptance and love of me."

The operative word is "freed." She's just going through her five steps. She's been freed from illusion and delusion. She's been freed from cynicism by his acceptance and love.

She also has a powerful final comment on her marriage, and marriage in general, and on life's passage, which is what I'm talking about. She says: "Our love has been anything but perfect and anything but static. Inevitably there have been times when one of us has outrun the other, and has had to wait patiently for the other to catch up. There have been times when we have misunderstood each other, demanded too much of each other, been insensitive to the other's needs. I do not believe there is any marriage in which this does not happen. The growth of love is not a straight line, but a series of hills and valleys. I suspect that in every good marriage there are times when love seems to be over. Sometimes those desert lines are simply the only way to the next oasis, which is far more lush and beautiful after the desert crossing than it could possibly have been without."

Isn't that lovely? It's about life, not just marriage. She knew she had to go through those desert lines and then the oasis turned out to be so much more beautiful. And that's exactly what Moses and Elijah were saying. Foolish Peter, who wanted to freeze the moment, like he was straight out of Madison Avenue, but Moses and Elijah said, and Jesus agreed, "There's another, better, more profound transfiguration, that comes only through the passage of those five steps."

Once you've been through the oasis, and once you learn to pray, and swallow your pride, you say, "I need a power greater than myself. I've got disappointment, and I've got hurt, and I've got bitterness, perhaps, but I realize now these can be a passage to the oasis, the transfiguration." As I said, many haven't reached that point. They're stuck in cynicism. Marriage is a fraud. The job's a fraud. Friendships are a fraud. These are people who got stuck on stage two. And they have to learn a little bit more, so let's pray for them; and pray for ourselves.

And next time you listen to this gospel, just don't think of the transfiguration as a magic show. Think of it as a profound statement about life. There's the ideal, but to achieve it in a different dimension, you must undergo a passage. You and I balk, and you and I don't want to go through that desert, but go we must, we have no choice. But we're not alone. We have each other. We have our faith community. And above all, we have the Jesus who's been through it all, who knows what it's about, and turns to us in his glory and says, "Come to me, all of you who are heavily ladened and burdened, and I will refresh your soul, for my burden is easy and my yoke is light."

6

✝

Good Samaritan

Luke 10:30–37

Most likely, for more years than we'd like to count, we've heard this gospel that we now call the Good Samaritan. But we have always listened to it, or read it, in terms of stereotypes, the stereotypes being that there are three bad guys—the lawyer, the priest, and the Levite. And there's one good guy, the Samaritan.

Perhaps it's time to rescue this gospel from that stereotyping because as a matter of fact, it really has something different to say, and is much more contemporary than we'd like to think, because basically, it's dealing with ethical and moral issues.

Let's start with the lawyer, who is a good guy. He is not trying to entrap Jesus, nor is he trying to make a fool of him. What he's doing was standard fare of that day. Jesus was an itinerant rabbi. As in the universities, the people would come up, particularly the lawyers, and they would pose questions, which was a part of the academic setting. Then they would all sit down and they would bounce the questions and the answers around, tapping the mind of the master to see what he would say. Much the same as they do in law schools today.

So the lawyer was not being sneaky, nor was he being evil;

31

he was simply asking a standard question. And in response, therefore, Jesus gives an answer, but he tosses the answer back to his audience, like a good teacher, and says basically, when you think of it, "We have some ethical and moral issues here that are not that clear, so let's think about them" And then he tells them the story of the man going from Jerusalem to Jericho; he was robbed, beaten, most of his clothes were taken, and he was left for dead.

The first one to come down the road was the priest. But the priest is a good guy, not as we're used to thinking of him; he isn't some insensitive clod. You have to look at the issues here. You have to remember that in those days the priest was charged with ministering to the people and offering the sacrifice in the temple. It was something that the whole community expected of him. More than that, in those days the priest was social security and welfare and medicaid all wrapped up in one person. He was the one who was the conduit for charities and care for people. People depended upon him.

Now there were certain things that would prevent him from doing his jobs, which the people needed him to perform. And one of those things, according to law, was to come within thirty steps of the dead. If he did that, or touched a dead body, he was made ritually unclean, and then he could not perform the prayers at the temple, and he was disqualified, for a good period of time, from his work. When you understand that, it puts the priest in a different light; he is no longer an insensitive clod. But there's a man lying there; he's dead as far as the priest can tell. He can't tell whether it's a fellow Jew because most of the man's clothes have been taken. If it were a non-Jew he wouldn't even think of going near him or wasting time on him, because to the Jews of that time a neighbor was only another Jew.

He was faced here with an ethical, moral question: "If I go over and just with my foot turn the body over just to make certain he's dead, and I become ritually unclean, then what good am I to the rest of my people? I can't help them, I can't service them. So many people will be hurt, or certainly disenfranchised, if I touch this body. The man's dead anyway. What more could I do?"

The chances are very good that 100 percent of the audience who was listening to the story agreed with the priest's decision. It was very eminently sensible. Why should he jeopardize so many people by touching a dead body which he could not help anyway?

But Jesus comes along in this discussion, and he opens the door to the possibility that the priest made a wrong ethical decision. Jesus suggests that the priest made a good decision, but that there was a better one. Jesus raises the possibility that although the priest would be legally unclean, and there were honest-to-goodness legal issues here that the priest had to consider, still there were other elements of the situation that had to be taken into account. Jesus offered compassion and love as factors that might bear upon the priest's decision and his moral quandary. So what you have here is a good man who is following the rules, and Jesus comes along and says, "There may be other ways to measure your conduct."

This is a very contemporary situation. For example, doing business today can put unbearable pressures upon people. The result is that often they're forced to act in ways that are inhumane and hurtful to others in order to close the deal, in order to close the contract, in order to make "X" number of dollars, in order to meet the deadlines, and for a host of other reasons. People are often sacrificed.

That is to say that people in our own society are treated as objects, or things, or pawns—and it's good business. But Jesus raises the ethical question: "But are good business and sensibleness the only measurements?" To be compassionate often doesn't make good economic sense. But that's the way love is.

Love often doesn't make sense.

The priest's dilemma is our dilemma every day, isn't it? Faced with a decision that'll be good for business but bad for human beings, we say, "Well, this is the sensible thing to do. If I don't do this, then people will lose their jobs, or the plant will lose money, people will be unemployed, so I kind of have to look the other way." You see, it's a moral dilemma. And the story is saying, "But Christians should have another measurement besides common sense. It should be compassion."

Next we have another good guy, the Levite. He comes down the road shortly after. He wasn't a priest. He was more like a deacon, or chairperson, or head of the parish council. He knew that the priest had gone ahead of him because in those days the roads were so dangerous they knew which roads were traveled, and in small villages like that, he knew the priest had just preceded him from the temple, maybe by half an hour.

So he comes along, and he sees the man who was apparently dead, and he thinks of himself, rightly, "Well, the priest went by and he didn't do anything, and he didn't think it was necessary to stop. And the priest is the priest, and he knows more than I do, and he's the boss. Why whould I stop?" Which is very good sense.

But you sense another contemporary problem, don't you? The Levite did not have authority. He deferred to the man who did. His tactic was to go along with someone else's judgment. If the person in authority over you makes a decision, then you just follow orders. What could be more reasonable? But Jesus comes along and says, "If you and I as Christians continue to use that excuse, then we'll continue to have concentration camps, we'll continue to have events like My Lai (soldiers who shot civilians 'because I was just following orders'). You will continue to have people use excuses that say, 'Hey, I'm looking the other way, but I'm not in charge.' "

If they're doing these horrible, despicable things at HUD,* and raking off billions of dollars from the poor who should get housing, and that comes from the top and my boss knows about it, then who am I to open my mouth? You know the story. If you're a whistle-blower, you are very liable to lose your job. This is the moral stance, isn't it? "That's not my depart-

---

*In the summer of 1989 a huge scandal involving bribes, cronyism, and mismanagement was uncovered inside the United States government's Department of Housing and Urban Development (HUD).

ment. I'm not in charge. I mean something wrong's going on in this plant, in this factory, in this profession. There are some bad, evil decisions being made, but, you know, I'm only the underling. I'm only the Levite. I'm following orders. Don't blame me." That was Eichmann's plea at the Nuremburg trials.

And Jesus says, "That's not good enough. Not good enough. That's not good enough." You see what's wrapped up in this story? It's not an evil Levite; it's a good Levite, who very sensibly said, "If my boss didn't bother, why should I?" But Jesus says, "There's got to be a better measurement than that."

Finally, we have the Samaritan. Well, he identified, I guess, with the body there because that was, figuratively, himself. He was an outcast. He was in a segregated society. He could touch the body fifty times—he'd be no worse off. The Jews hated him, considered him unclean. And whether he helped or not wouldn't change his status one bit with the Jews. They thought the Samaritans were wretched people anyway. So mentioning that, Jesus brings up the whole issue of prejudice. And the audience would squirm at that.

Anyway, Jesus comes back to the question. "Now, who was neighbor to the one who was robbed?" The lawyer's reluctant admission is it must be the Samaritan, but his legal mind says the priest and the Levite were right. And Jesus has to concur. As far as they went, they were right. But what Jesus proposes is that we have to go farther.

That's what's in this gospel. It's a gospel about ethics and morals. It's a gospel that says that compassion comes over the rule, and love is over the law, and integrity is over authority. And to live that way is to live a profoundly Christ-like life. Be ready to take the consequences of that.

Most of us accommodate, don't we? And most of us excuse our behavior because "that's not my job." And most of us turn the other way because "that's not my responsibility." And most of us plead good common sense, like the priest. And there's a lot of merit to that. But the radicalness of the gospel says that we don't, or should not, live like other people. It's a beautiful and costly thing to be a Christian.

And if you were the priest, as good as he was, he followed the rules, you should have, in this instance, said, "The heck with the rules," and showed compassion. And if you were the Levite, good man that he was, you should not hide behind the excuse that "The boss didn't do anything, so I guess I don't have to do anything either." Jesus says, "You have to jeopardize something to be a disciple."

So the next time you hear the story of the Good Samaritan, listen with new ears. Not with the old stereotypes of two lousy bums and one noble character. No, that gets us off the hook. We are talking about two fine, outstanding, honest people—three, including the lawyer. But all of them are being challenged by Jesus to go beyond the law, to go beyond the excuse, to go beyond the authority; and to come down to that love which expresses itself in compassion, and invites all of us to be Good Samaritans.

7

Central Park

John 17:20–25

Let us together, this morning, in the light of the gospel, reflect on Central Park.*

What happened in Central Park, of course, is a horrible thing. And the media have not let us forget the horror. It is difficult for us even to imagine what those rampaging youths did to an innocent bystander. The violence, the hatred, the sexual abuse, all that sent shivers up and down our spines.

It is interesting, however, as you read the press and listen to the media, to notice the interpretations that they give this. They talk about these boys being poor, and this girl working for some bank, or whatever, representing "yuppie-ville" and all that the boys are distanced from. Or there is talk about these boys being disenfranchised from society and taking their vengeance and their frustration out on the woman. Or there are hints of racism, although they try hard to downplay that because of its volatility and sensitivity. And so on and so on.

But you can't help but notice how the sociological and the psychological terminology is used with as much conviction

---

*In the early summer of 1989 a group of rampaging ("wilding") boys attacked and raped a woman jogger in Central Park in New York City. The incident and its aftermath were widely reported in the media.

and cant as the worst of medieval speculation. The public pro-
hibition against any religious categories as at least one among
several approaches is very noticeable.

George Will, the columnist, with whom I don't always
agree, had an interesting column on this Central Park thing.
He remarked: "Various experts say they know why this happened. Alienation, anomie, boredom, rage, raging boredom,
peer pressure, inequality, status anxiety, television, advertising. We have here another triumph of the social science of vic-
timology. Its specialty is the universalization of victimhood.
The dispersal of responsibility into a fog of socio-economic factors. In earlier times, descriptions of an episode like the one in
Central Park would have begun with a judgment that today is
never reached at all. The attackers did what they did because
they are evil. Today the people respond, 'Evil? Such a primi-
tive notion; not at all useful as an explanation.' But that response is not real sophisticiation, it is a form of flinching. It is a
failure of nerve. A vanishing moral vocabulary is being replaced by academic rubbish, collected reflectively by serious
newspapers."

Now please understand me, especially those of you in these
disciplines. The insights of sociology and psychology are extremely helpful and useful, and we're grateful for them, but
when their language is the only officially permitted language,
when as George Will comments, the moral vocabulary vanish-
es, and when in fact, religious discourse and wisdom are
drummed out of court, then as far as these boys go, they can't
be healed, they can only be modified.

They can't be redeemed, they can only be programmed.
They can't be saved, they can only be incarcerated. They can't
be forgiven, they can only be psychoanalyzed. They can't be
judged, they can only be sentenced. They can't be prayed for,
they can only be analyzed. They can't be introduced to repentance, but only introduced to therapy. They can't be told of an
unconditional, all-embracing love that went to the cross, but
only be told, "Have a nice day."

Not for these boys to be the prodigal sons falling into the

arms of a forgiving Father; rather they can only be adolescents sitting across the desk from their social worker. It's good, but it's not good enough. Not good enough. As Wall Street is learning, as Harvard is learning, as public education is learning—tossing out religious categories and trying to manage with what's left over is simply not good enough.

Evil and God; sin and redemption; good and bad; light and darkness; angels and demons; mercy and justice; repentance and forgiveness; heaven and hell—these are still valuable metaphors. And even though such messages in the past have forged their tyrannies and fears, in their best moments they have held out wholeness and newness of life. For a Paul, who while his hands were still red with Stephen's blood, could be knocked from his horse and gaze into the face of the risen Christ. For a Magdalene, who could be called from her sexual sin, and look into the eyes of Pity. For an Augustine, who could pick up the Scriptures and wend his way to Milan and fall at the feet of Ambrose, and make his confession and be restored. For a Dorothy Day, who was called from her atheism and communism, and became an apostle for Jesus Christ. For a Thomas Merton, wondering what he was doing in his wickedness, on his knees in a Catholic church in Greenwich Village, gazing at the statue of Christ. A Malcolm Muggeridge, a playboy, who became a convert because in Mother Teresa he saw something of the divine. Charles Colson, a convicted felon, who served Jesus in his fellow prisoners. And a John Newton whose hymn we sing—slave trader and woman abuser—who celebrates his conversion to Jesus in "Amazing Grace."

I guess what I'm saying for us believers is that Central Park is not just a question of race, poverty, and economics, although these may be factors. It is also a story of divisions within the human heart, which cries out for redemption and repentance, renewal, and a God so wide, so big, so strong, so caring, so loving that this God can take on our flesh, can embrace little children, can eat with sinners, can forgive "good thieves," and can promise eternal life to those who love this God.

And so the ending words to this morning's gospel are very

apropos to Central Park. They are words that must be in our hearts, we can say to these wilding boys and adolescents: "For all the help you can get from the social scientists, and indeed, that help is good, we offer another dimension. We offer you forgiveness in the Lord Jesus. We offer you the embrace of the prodigal's father. We offer you the chance of newness of life."

So it is in our hearts that the closing words of the gospel make sense: "Just Father, the world has not known you. And these have known that you sent me. To them I have revealed your name, and I will continue to reveal it so that your love for me may live in them, and I may live in them."

This is the good news that you and I have, and what brings us to worship this Sunday morning. And although we shudder at what happened in Central Park, we know that there is more of an answer than public discourse will allow. There is an answer of faith that is legitimate.

Perhaps these boys, most of all, are crying out for a redeemer more than for a therapist. For a knowledge of a God who loves them as wildly as they abuse others. But someone has to tell them that. Maybe they need to hear from us, a faith community, that there is such a thing as repentance, that their terrible sin doesn't have to cripple their lives until they die. And that being put behind bars is not the only form of imprisonment.

So Central Park touches our lives, not because we fear that we may be abused some day and be the object of such terribleness; it touches our lives because as people who are gathered here around the word of God, we have something to say about Central Park, and we have someone to point to concerning Central Park, and we have something to live in our lives that will tell our sons and daughters that there's a better way both to live and to love.

8

The Persistence of Mary

Luke 8:19–21

I want to explore why Mary has been so persistently important through the twenty centuries that we have been around as a people of God. I'm interested not just in why we identify with her, but also in why she persists through the ages. To begin to get an answer to this question I'd like to go down a kind of litany of her role as found in Scripture.

The first thing we get from Scripture, particularly from St. Luke, is that Mary is the first disciple and she remains faithful. Luke makes this point by telling us that when the angel comes and asks Mary to become the mother of the messiah, she says "yes" and then remains faithful to that "yes" even in the most difficult of times.

So Luke says this about Mary: she was the first believer in Jesus; she was the first follower; the first disciple; and she didn't fall away in troubled times. And if for no other reason, she thus earned a mark of respect in the early church community.

Secondly, in the gospel, Mary is revealed as someone who keeps God's word. I don't know if you remember that incident when Mary and her relatives were trying to see Jesus, who was in the full bloom of his public ministry, and there was a big mob around him. So they sent word through the mob, and they said, "Well, Jesus, your mother and your relatives are here." And Jesus made this response. He said, "But who is my mother, my father, my brother and sister? The one who keeps the will of God. That's my mother, and my brother, and my sister." And in effect what he was saying was that Mary's claim to greatness was not that she was his biological mother, but that she kept the word of God. And that's a remarkable compliment to this persistent woman.

Thirdly, here's where she gets closer to us. She becomes a representative of all the silenced witnesses and members of the exploited class. Remember, Mary lived in occupied territory. She knew what the Palestinians or the black Africans know today. She knew segregation, she knew a minority place, she knew what it was to be a woman. She had to keep her mouth shut while Herod killed the innocent children of Bethlehem. She had to stand on the fringe of the crowd while she saw her son publicly humiliated, carrying the cross. She had to stand behind the soldiers' spears that formed a fence, and she could not get to Jesus on the cross to give him some comfort.

And that's why people have always related to Mary in the great Pieta, holding the broken body of her son; people can identify with her letting forth the only thing she was permitted to let forth—a cry and a scream, and hard tears. Those who are oppressed and cannot speak out because they'll be imprisoned or shot, or retribution will be made against their families, they understand Mary. And she understands them.

Any parent who's worried about pornography; any parents who are worried about people coming up to their children and pushing drugs; and parents who are looking at the values of the media, which are horrendous, and who say, "We don't want to live like that," but are powerless and helpless to control these things. You know what Mary means, and why she persists—because we can identify with that woman who is the silenced witness to things that are better; and society keeps her suppressed.

Fourthly, Mary is a faith pilgrim. And people can certainly

identify with that. Remember the story in Luke? The angel said, "You are to be the mother of God." And what did she say? She asked the question, "How can this be?" And how many people throughout the ages, including you and me, have cried that? How can I tackle this challenge? How can I survive? How can I begin all over again as a widow?

We tend to romanticize the fact that Mary was married to Joseph and she lost him somewhere along the way. But there's no romance in losing a spouse, as those of you who are widows and widowers know. Or losing a child in crucifixion. Knowing death and separation. Being a bereaved person.

And you ask Mary's question, "How can this be?" You ask: "How can I carry on? How can I survive life? How can I get along? I don't know what I'm going to do. I've just been told I have cancer. I've just been told I have a short time to live. I've just lost my job. How can this be?" You are asking Mary's question, "How can this be?" No wonder Mary persists. We identify with her questioning.

Next, Scripture says that Mary is the keeper of memories. Remember what St. Luke says? She didn't understand these things, but Mary treasured all these things in her heart. So as other marauders come in and destroy books and destroy monuments, and destroy photographs and destroy names, and destroy values, you look to the valiant men and women who keep the memories and treasures in their hearts, people who someday will retell our story to us when we've forgotten it. No wonder oppressed people identify with Mary, the keeper of memories—they look to her because the oppressors have tried to erase the people's names and stories out of the history books.

Next, Mary is a model of simplicity. And I think part of her power in history is due to this, because as we get all these very elaborate liturgies, and all of these very elaborate doctrines, and all of these very elaborate regulations, somehow Mary cuts through all that, and when people are crying or on their sick bed, they simply say, "Ave Maria." It's as simple as that. So she becomes just a model of simplicity that cuts through a great deal.

Next, Mary is the God-bearer, and of course, that is our role. She gave forth to the world the living Christ, and I think people through the ages have always identified with that role. They say, "This is my role." Everyone here is to be a Christ-bearer, to birth the Lord and give him to other people. Mary did that, and so we recognize that. We have a kindred spirit there.

And finally, I think Mary persists because she has been given to us. Remember the scene on Calvary? Jesus is dying. There's his mother. "Who will take care of my mother when I'm gone?" So he turns to John, who represents all the Christian family, and says, "Son, behold thy mother." And he gives away his last, and his most precious possession. And we are the recipients of that. And that's why Luke has Mary stand up in the temple and sing her Magnificat and her great prophecy: "Behold, all generations shall call me blessed."

And so, from the very outlandish to the very simple, Mary becomes significant, and her prophecy comes true. Whether it's Our Lady of Guadalupe, Lourdes, Fatima, or Medjugorje, you name it, however you feel about these things, behind these appearances, behind the shrines, behind even the gross exaggerations, is a woman who won't go away. Simply because she is just enormously human, because she is enormously a great disciple, and because everything in her life has touched our lives.

There's not a tear or a smile of Mary's that we haven't felt. There's not a question and a hurt and a pain and a suffering that we can't identify with. No wonder she persists.

9

✛

Trinity:

A Matter of Relationship

Matthew 28:16–20

For Catholics, since time immemorial, the Trinity has been a symbol of the most difficult conundrum that we could wrestle with.

I'd like to give you a different perspective on the Trinity. I'm not going to try to explain it, because if we're forthright about it, we have to admit it can't really be explained. I'm merely going to try to put it in perspective, and then see what it suggests to us.

Because the topic is a tough one, let me start off with a little tough quotation from a Scottish philosopher, John McMurray. Listen as I read this, and then I'll try to unfold it. He wrote this about fifty years ago, and he's been really validated since, particularly and interestingly through the sciences, both physics and psychology. He says, "The theme we have to expound and sustain is that the self is constituted by relation to the other."

Infants, for example, are made to be cared for. They are born in a love relationship which is inherently personal. Not merely their personal development, but their very survival depends upon maintaining the relationship they depend on for their existence; that is to say upon intelligent understanding, upon rational forethought. They cannot think for themselves, yet they cannot do without thinking. For human infants, and this is the heart of the matter, the impulse to communication is their sole adaptation to the world in which they are born. Implicit and unconscious as it may be, yet it is sufficient to constitute the mother-child relationship in the basic form of human existence as personal mutuality.

All of infants' subsequent experience, all the habits they form and skills they acquire, fall within the framework of a personal relationship. Thus, human experience is, in principle, shared experience. Human life, even its most individual elements, is a common life, and human behavior carries always in its inherent structure a reference to the personal other. All this may be summed up by saying that the unit of personal existence is not the individual, but two persons in personal relationship; and that we are persons, not by individual right, but in virtue of our relationship to another. The personal is constituted by personal relations. The unit of the personal is not the "I" but the "you and I."

What does this philosopher mean? He means what we know and experience—that none of us exists on our own. We exist only in relationship to something else. What makes us truly human is not, as they would have us believe, some kind of hedonistic "I." The essence of a human being is to be in relation to the other. The relationship is what constitutes our existence and our wholeness. Let's bring this to a practical matter. Think for a moment—what are your best moments? Your really best moments? Now however you spell it out to me, the bottom line of everyone's best moment is this: when we were in relationship. Isn't that true? When my mother hugged me— my best moment. When my lover embraced me. When someone who cared for me was in the same room with me. When my teacher affirmed me. When friendship was valuable and touchable and strong. We remember those as our best moments, and they were moments when we were in relation.

We resonate, for example, with little historical tidbits like this: General Grant, as you probably know, had a very close friend named John Rawlins, who was a lawyer. If you go to Washington, right in front of the Capitol you see the statue of General Grant astride his horse, with all the great scenes of battle beside him.

As you may know, Grant had a terrible drinking problem. He was an alcoholic, and the only friend who was really close to him in his life was this man, John Rawlins. It was John Rawlins who got him to take the pledge to stay sober, particularly in a terrible war; he had so many people who were dependent on him to live. And when Grant fell off the wagon and went back to drinking, it was John Rawlins who went to him as a friend, confronted him, and reminded him once more how many people depended on him.

Beyond these facts about this relationship there is something very interesting. As I said, if you go to Washington, you can look in front of the Capitol and you'll see Grant on his horse. But if you go down Pennsylvania Avenue, down to the other end, south of the Capitol, you will find a park called Rawlins Park.

In that park is a very nondescript statue of John Rawlins. Knowing this story, I thought it was of great significance. When I looked at the statue of John Rawlins, my eye traveled over to see General Grant and knew that literally and figuratively, the only reason Grant stayed on his horse was because of John Rawlins. That's true, isn't it?—Grant's best moment was when he was in relationship to a friend. We resonate with that story. Being with somebody is the height of what life's about, we say.

This is Memorial Day weekend, and at least in part it is meant as a time for us to remember those who died in war fighting for the United States. And, like other holidays, it's also a time for visiting others. Why will you be visiting? Because, instinctively, without thinking about it, there's something written in your nature and mine that says you must "be with"— that's the essence of life. Whether we visit the dead by going to the cemetery, remember those who have given their lives for our country, or we visit the living. When we are ill, we want somebody to be with us, don't we? Somebody to care. Somebody to acknowledge our sickness.

I don't know if you saw that very lovely film, just a marvelous thing, *There Were Times, Dear.* Remember that? I think Joanne Woodward played in it. Such a great actress. It was a story of a woman who had to cope with the progressive Alzheimer's disease of her husband. The film shows her watching him get more and more lost; she watches him become dazed and become a drooling invalid; she worries when she wakes up in the morning and he's missing and she doesn't know where in the neighborhood he is. But she doesn't keep her distance. The film shows that she stays with him, she cares for him, she bathes him, and she dresses him. And she does all of this with the knowledge that he will not only never be the same again, but there will come a point when he will not even know who she is. And the last scene I remember too poignantly is when she was tying a bib on her husband and feeding him pablum. She had no thought that she would leave him or divorce him or stay away. I found the story so moving and it resonated within me, as I am sure it would within you, because underneath, theologically and philosophically, it was a true statement about who she was and who he was. They had to be in relationship. Even people who are dying need to be in relationship. They're not so much afraid of death; they're afraid of dying alone.

When I read that book about "the winter of life," the story of old people in nursing homes, that was the recurring theme. They weren't afraid of death. As one old gentleman said, "I don't want to die alone like a sparrow in a winter hedge—at least have somebody with me to tell me that I mattered. I must be in relationship."

Again, I think that's why all of us a few years ago were moved by that very powerful film, *Brian's Song.* Remember? It was about Brian Piccolo, who got cancer, and Gayle Sayres, the great football player. Gayle, of course, is black, and Brian is white; and in all of professional sports history they were the first black man, and white man to room together. All the world and the reporters were watching this carefully to see how this black man and this white man would get along together. Of course, what kept them together was their great sense of humor. I remember reading in the story that when they asked Brian Piccolo, "How do you two get along? How is it living with a black man?" he said, "It's okay as long as he doesn't use the bathroom." It's that kind of humor.

Of course when Brian got cancer, he wasn't able to take part in the great playoffs, and finally Gayle Sayres won the most important of the awards, the George S. Halas Award. Do you remember when he stood up in front of everybody to accept the award? (And remember Gayle Sayres is a man who has said about two words in public in his whole life.) He said this, and I would like to quote him. He said, "You flatter me by giving me this award; but I tell you here and now that I accept it for Brian Piccolo. Brian Piccolo is the man of courage who should receive the George S. Halas Award. I love Brian Piccolo, and I'd like you to love him. Tonight when you hit your knees, please ask God to love him too."

Why did that move us? Not because it was just an extraordinary friendship of a black and a white man, but because he was able to say something about relationship, "I love this man," and right away we resonate, because imprinted in us is that's who we are. We're at our best in relationship, and you flip it over to the other side, this is where we are least ourselves—when we are out of relationship. The worst pain and illness in the world is what? To be out of relationship. What do they do when they want to punish somebody severely? They put the person in solitary confinement. Those of you who have been through the pain of divorce know that deep down the pain is to have a failed relationship, however it happened. Alienation is a word we give that. Unforgiveness. And that's why people have such a cry and a need for what? Forgiveness and reconciliation.

So what's the point of it all? The point of it all is simply this. These experiences are universal experiences that tell us about ourselves. They tell us that not only do we exist (animals exist, trees exist), but we exist in relationship. Relationship is what makes us what we truly are, and now we have to ask the big question: Why? And the Feast of the Holy Trinity is the answer. Because we are made in the image and the likeness of God, and that is ultimately the meaning of today's feast.

The Trinity is a revelation that says relationship is what God is—no wonder you are imprinted with this, as if it's stuck into your neural system. God is Father, Son, and Holy Spirit, and no matter what else that means, it certainly is essentially relationship. What makes God God is relationship . However you explain it, whatever the philosophers and theologians do, really doesn't interest us here. The whole impact of the revelation is this: Relationship is what God is about, and therefore it is no wonder that we, who are made in God's image and likeness, are also essentially about relationship.

No wonder when the angel announced that God would become a man, he said that you shall call him what? *Emmanuel,* which is the Hebrew word for "God with us." No wonder Jesus said, "I no longer call you servants, but I call you friends." No wonder that in today's special gospel he said, "I am with you all days even to the end of the world." So if we want to know about this very esoteric feast of the Trinity, I suggest that the Trinity sheds light on five realities.

Number One: The Trinity sheds light on our nature. Who are we? We are a people who have a desperate, desperate, desperate drive to be in relationship, and we are happiest when we are. Isn't that true? Secondly, the Trinity shows us the primacy of love. If God is in relationship, it is a love relationship, and no wonder the poets and songwriters, ever since human beings have been on the planet, have been struggling with this thing, love, because essentially we're struggling with ourselves.

Thirdly, the Trinity says this is the image we are and that's why we are baptized in the name of the Father and of the Son and of the Holy Spirit, because the baptism says this is who you are in relationship to me.

Fourthly, the Trinity is a basis of hope. Remember your old catechism question, "Why did God make us?" God made us to know, to love, and to serve God in this world, and to be happy with God forever in the next. Now that you're big people, the operative word is "with." The end of human existence is to be in relationship with a God who made us in God's image.

Finally, the Trinity explains our restlessness. The Trinity explains that without your lover near you, you are restless, and that's why you've got to go see Grandmom today or that's why you are going to see your sweetheart. You can't tolerate to be separated, and you call people up if you are really in love. The restlessness is explained by St. Augustine's famous words, "Thou has made us for thyself, O God, and we are restless until we rest in thee." So if we're edgy about existence, it's because heaven's going to be meeting our lover.

It's all going to connect, and the Trinity is about all that, you see. It's not a mathematical question; it's not even a theological question in the sense of the theologian. It is a Valentine question. So the next time you say you believe in the Father, Son, and the Holy Spirit, and the next time somebody says, "Well, you're a Catholic; you believe in the Trinity; what is it all about?"—don't go into long philosophical discussions. Say: "It's about me and it's about God, and it's about relationships. I can't say more than that, but I know in my heart, it's about image. I am who I am because God is who God is, and that's the best I can say about the Trinity."

10

✝

Love Trusts

Matthew 11:25–30

Some time ago, twenty-three-year-old Patrick Purdy killed five small children in a schoolyard. And then he turned the gun on himself and took his own life.

So I ask you to imagine, however difficult it is because it's so uncomfortable, I ask you to imagine that you are the parent of one of those slain children. You run down the litany of the feelings you absolutely have to have gotten: total shock, and disbelief; and grief and horror; and then, of course, finally rage.

But if that weren't bad enough, there is one more pain, which is probably the worst of all—and that is you can't even vent your rage on anyone because the young man was irresponsible; he was psychotic; but worse than that—he is dead.

So you think of that. There's no place to put your anger, no place to release your hate. There's nobody's chest that you can pound; there's not even an idiot face that you can yell at. There's no human being left that you can curse. There's no one around that you can even prosecute or that you can imprison. It's extremely unfair, to say the least. There's just raw frustration, with no place to go; except you can go inward and poison your system, or it can deteriorate your health. And, of course, there's always the third outlet—God.

I thought of this when I heard Friday of the death of Bill Johnson, who was jogging along at Brookdale College—he was the athletic director, in good health. And not only did he just drop dead, but it was a year ago that his own young son died of a brain tumor. And so you listen to things like that, and read stories of five innocent children slain playing in their schoolyard, and then you ask, if not out loud, how do you square that with God?

And I think the question gets extremely poignant when you add, How do you square these things with God, especially when you have been good, and you have kept the commandments; and feel, rightly so, that after all, you deserve some consideration? You can't help but think that a God who does not come across for the faithful ones is either pretty fickle or pretty powerless. Now that's understandable.

But I think these incidents and the light of St. Paul's Scripture [1 Corinthians 13] force us to the deep question, the question that you and I don't like to look at because, again, it's not a terribly comfortable question; and it's very challenging, and goes right to the heart of the matter. Beneath all these tragedies and anger, and rage and perplexity, is the question that sooner or later we have to try to wrestle with, and that is: What is your relationship with God?

And the only way to respond to that is to say, "Well, what is my relationship with other people?" Fundamentally, we all have to say that my relationship with other people has to at least try to rest on some kind of a trust, even in perplexing and strained times; and maybe *especially* in perplexing and strained times. We accept, without question, that our relationships with other human beings are not a "tit for tat" contract type of thing: "I will be loyal and so will you. I will be honest and so will you. I will be faithful and so will you. I will do everything I should and so will you." It just doesn't happen that neatly, does it? It just doesn't happen that way.

And because it doesn't, and because we know that relationships are imperfect, and are not based on guarantees but on trust, we make considerable room for forgiveness and reconciliation; for change and growth; for uncertainty; for hope; and, ultimately, as St. Paul says, for love—a love that somehow will overcome all the deficiencies.

But when it comes to our relationship with God, we change the rules, don't we? You think about that. We come up with this extremely odd "contract" notion. "God, I kept all the commandments, so how could you let my daughter get sick? How could you let my marriage fail, and disintegrate and break up? How could you let my innocent child get machine-gunned at school? How *could* you?"

It always amazes me when Christians say things like *that*, although I can understand it when they're under stress. For after all, Christians every single year celebrate a two-thousand-year-old story of a man who was faithful to God, who kept all the commandments, and who wound up being spit upon, and stripped, and scourged, and crowned with thorns, and hung on a cross to die; and this was one about whom God said, "This is my beloved son."

But anyway, what gets exposed here is the one-dimensional shallowness of our relationship with God, which we would not tolerate with other people. When we analyze it, our relationship with God is one of contract, not of trust. With God, somehow, we want not trust, but guarantee; not acceptance, but explanation; not faith, but certainty; not adventure, but predictability; not ambiguity, but a flow chart; not mystery, but a signed contract. Is that the way you treat other people in your life? Why do we do it to God?

Or are we ready to trust that God, being God, will have the last word in all the madness and absurdities of life as God did in the absurdity and madness of what happened to God's beloved son? And even there, what's our view of Jesus? I have a feeling that for most of us it's a distorted view: Jesus is the great detached one, who up his sleeve had the master plan laid out, and he says, "Well, I can put up with a little bit of fuss because in the end we're all going to live happily ever after."

But the fact is that Jesus was not the great detached one. If anything, Jesus comes across in the Scripture as the great pilgrim, the authentic life who did not escape the human condition; who did not know the master plan; who did not have the completed script; who took life day by day and let life's evil have its full play while his Father, who would not remove human freedom with all its potential for good and evil, wept at what happened to him.

And in the end, the Father dried his tears and raised Jesus up, as Jesus trusted that he would, although he had his last minute doubts: "My God, my God, why have you forsaken me?" That's faith. Faith is belief surrounded by doubt, with doubt getting stronger in troubled times. But that's relationship. Just like husbands and wives, and brothers and sisters, and friends and lovers; with all the unfairness of life, you have to trust—or you die.

Let me share with you the true story of a soldier named Joseph Schultz. Just over one hundred years ago Adolph Hitler was born. In his fifty-six years on the planet he did incredible harm and was responsible for millions of terrible deaths. Yet in all of the horror that he unleashed, there are pinpoints of light and nobility. And this German soldier, Joseph Schultz, who was the same age as Patrick Purdy, who machine-gunned children in the schoolyard, was one of these pinpoints.

He was sent to Yugoslavia shortly after the invasion. He was a loyal, young German soldier on patrol, and one day the sergeant called out eight names, his among them. They thought they were going on a routine patrol, and as they hitched up their rifles, they came over a hill, still not knowing what their mission was. There were eight Yugoslavians there, standing on the brow of the hill; five men and three women. It was only when they got about fifty feet away from them, when any marksman could shoot out an eye of a pheasant, that the soldiers realized what their mission was.

The eight soldiers were lined up. The sergeant barked out, "Ready!" and they lifted up their rifles. "Aim," and they got their sights. And suddenly in the silence that prevailed, there was a thud of a rifle butt against the ground. The sergeant, and the seven other soldiers, and those eight Yugoslavians stopped and looked. And Private Joseph Schultz walked toward the Yugoslavians. His sergeant called after him and ordered him to come back, but he pretended not to hear him.

Instead he walked the fifty feet to the mound of the hill, and he joined hands with the eight Yugoslavians. There was a moment of silence, then the sergeant yelled, "Fire!" And Private Joseph Schultz died, mingling his blood with those innocent men and women. What was found on his body was an excerpt from today's reading from St. Paul. The excerpt was: "Love does not delight in evil, but rejoices in the truth. It always protects, always trusts, always hopes, and always perseveres."

Private Joseph Schultz was drawn into a war that was absurd. He was drawn into an event that was evil, that he did not understand. He was drawn into a perplexity and an unfairness of life and he wondered what God could possibly have in mind. And yet he trusted that his sacrifice would make a difference, and that God would be faithful.

He had no guarantee. He had no special insight into any master plan. He had no assuredness, he only had a relationship with God, whom he trusted, even when he did not understand God. And I think that is what Paul is saying.

There is hardly anyone hearing this who cannot say life has been unfair. Many of you are in a broken relationship; some of your children have bitterly disappointed you; others among you are dying of cancer. And you say, "Life is unfair," and you're right. And you say, "I've been faithful. I go to church every Sunday and I follow all the rules. How could God do this to me? I've lost a relationship. I've lost a son. I've lost a spouse. I've lost a parent. I've lost a job. I've lost health. Is this the way God treats God's beloved ones?"

And all that I ask you to do as you get angry at God, is, for heaven's sake, look at the crucifix. This is his beloved son. In the crucifix is the message that you trust the relationship, as Jesus had to do. It is permissible to get angry, and it is permissible to doubt, as Jesus did on the cross. But in the end you have to ask, what is your relationship with God? If it's a relationship of a contract, you have a right to abandon God and say, "You didn't keep your part of the bargain, and I'm not keeping mine. Goodbye. I've had it!"

But if it's a relationship, like with somebody you love, then you have to trust God. With people you love, even though you don't understand what they're doing and why they're doing it, or why they're acting that way, you stick with them, even when they're mentally and emotionally and physically ill; you hang in there even when you see no end and no light at the end of the tunnel. God asks for nothing less than that. God is friend, is beloved, is in relationship with you, and like in any relationship, God asks for your trust. The resurrection of Jesus Christ, who had his doubts, is proof that God will have the last word.

So St. Paul is right, and Private Schultz is right, and Jesus is right. If God is love, love does not delight in evil; but love rejoices in the truth. Love always protects; love always trusts; love always hopes. And love always perseveres.

11

✝

The Gestures of Hope

Luke 7:11–17

I have to contemplate further that on the day I had a bad throat, no lector showed up. Shows God has a sense of humor.

It's an interesting gospel, depending how you want to look at it. One way to look at it is that here is Jesus coming along, and he raises someone from the dead. And then we say, "All right, that's a wonderful thing, and hopefully he'll do the same for me someday; and those who are near and dear to me." But he never does.

And so we say, "What does the gospel mean? Jesus raises people from the dead, and I've lost my children, my spouse, my parents, my siblings."

Let's put the gospel in perspective. As far as we can know, and from what the record says, there are only three people that Jesus raised from the dead. One was Jairus's daughter, one was this young man of Naim, and the other one was Lazarus. And apparently there were lots and lots of other people in his time and place and town who died. So if he didn't raise all of them up, but only two or three, we have to approach the gospel from another angle.

And the angle simply says this: that Jesus did not come to do away with death. He was to find that out for himself. But rather to tell us that God's compassion and power reach out to us, in and beyond death, and that therefore, ultimately, God's love will overcome. So what becomes important is not that Jesus might have raised this young man from the dead; but rather what becomes critical in his gesture, pointing to the love that is concerned, and that will conquer. And that's the gospel lesson for us.

For today, for all of our advanced civilization, we live in an age that is incredibly violent. Drugs and crime; and murder and divorce; and hunger and war; and hatred, and greed; and whole litany of things. What we need, therefore, are gestures of hope, signs of life, and hints of victory. And this is what the meaning of the gospel is. Jesus didn't raise everyone from the dead, but two or three, to be a gesture of hope, a sign of life, and a hint of victory.

Right now up in Newark, New Jersey, there's a group of Mother Teresa's sisters, living in kind of a crummy apartment there. They would be this gospel. They're not relieving all the hurt and all of the drugs and all of the hunger. But by their presence and their charity they are a gesture of hope, a sign of hope, and a hint of ultimate victory.

Many years ago, when Beverly Sills made her debut, she received a final ovation of eighteen minutes. Her little daughter was standing there and asked her father, "Was Mommy good?" She could surmise that Mommy was good because she could see the people applauding, but she could not hear them, for as you know, Beverly Sills's daughter was born totally deaf. She has another child, a son who is autistic to the point that he remains severely retarded. And yet those of you who know Beverly Sills and her nickname, Bubbles, know she remains in this terrible tragedy of her two children by her joy, by her reaching out in charity; she is a gesture of hope, a sign of life, and a sign of ultimate victory.

I think of Bill Wilson, the co-founder of AA, and certainly he didn't lick all of the addictions in the world. But by his concern and love he remains that sign of help as Jesus did in raising this young man at Naim.

Or perhaps more recently you and I were fascinated watching this young student dressed in white, at Beijing,* halting a whole column of tanks that could easily have run him over (we all saw that footage), until he was dragged away. Did he think he could make a difference? He did. Has he made a difference? Oh, by all means. People will look at that, and review that, and talk about that for time to come, and it will remain for those who seek freedom in China, a hint of victory and a sign of hope. What that young man in white did there, in front of the tanks, was precisely what Jesus was intending to do when he raised the widow's son.

It comes down to this. The message is that we don't have to be super-heroes, but we do have to be heroic to some degree by, as they say, saying "No!" to drugs, by returning found money, by trying to be decent people, or just by coming to church here. It doesn't mean that we're perfect or better than others, but it is an important gesture. That there's something more to life; and Someone more.

These are gestures that are full of promise, of repentance, and of healing. And so even though we can truthfully say, "Oh my God, there is so much crime and violence and terribleness in the world," we shouldn't let that make us cynical. The gospel is meant to say it is only those who have no faith who collapse and become cynical in the face of so much evil. So once in a while you have to make a gesture.

And so of all the deaths in Palestine, through compassion Jesus made this gesture. Not to take everyone's death away, but to remind us that death is not the last word. Not to say that death is not an evil that will be overcome by love, not to say that widows will no longer cry, but to say that the tears will be wiped away some day and joy will be given.

And we are invited into that gospel. We are invited not to look at it as a miracle story that happened two thousand years ago, angrily or secretly wishing Jesus would do the same for us. On the contrary, the gospel was written that we might do the same for Jesus.

---

*Site of a student uprising, cruelly suppressed, in 1989.

There's an old Indian story about a twelve-year-old boy who died of snake bite. The poison took away his life and his grieving parents carried his body to the holy man and laid it before him. And the three of them sat around the body sadly for a long, long time. Then the father finally arose from his grieving, went over to his child, stretched out his hands over the feet of the child, and said, "In all my life I have not worked for my family as I should have." And the poison left the feet of the child. Then the mother rose and she stretched her hands over the heart of the child, and she said, "In all my life I have not loved my family as I should." And the poison left the heart of the child. And the holy man stretched out his hands over the head of the dead boy and he said, "In all my life I have not believed the words I have spoken." And the poison left the head of the child. The child rose up, and the parents and the holy man rose up, and the village rejoiced that day.

That's what the gospel is about. We make gestures, we individuals. We don't think we're going to cure the entire world. But God has called you and me for a purpose. By divine providence you and I live in this time, in this place, and this moment of history; and everyone of us has the power to stop death somewhere along the way, and make a gesture of compassion and hope, don't we?

Everyone of us has the power to write a note, to pick up a telephone, to utter a word of forgiveness, to stroke another's face, to say "I love you," and to hug our children. The greatest power in the world.

So listen to the gospel anew. It's the gesture that counts. The sign of hope that counts. The hint of everlasting life, and the motion of ultimate victory. Jesus did that in his time. We are invited to do it in our time.

12

✝

Under the Broom Tree

1 Kings 19:1–9

One of the things that I did, as many tourists do, when I was up in New England a while back, was to visit some of the eighteenth-century church graveyards. I learned that the people who cut those gravestones knew that they would be seen, which is why they are so beautifully done. I further found out that in those days before television and Bruce Springsteen, this is what people did on a Sunday afternoon. They walked through the cemeteries reading the inscriptions.

The most common inscription was one that was imported from Europe and translated; and this I found and jotted down as the one we saw most. It says, "Behold and see as you pass by, / As you are now so once was I. / As I am now so you will be, / Prepare for death and follow me." So that's to the point, isn't it?

Others, I think unintentionally, didn't realize some of the humor that they had there. For example, one I copied down says, "Here lies the body of Obadiah Wilkinson and Ruth, his wife; their warfare is accomplished." One says this: "She lived with her husband fifty years and died in a confident hope of a better life." Way before Madison Avenue, some enterprising eighteenth-century man has this on his wife's tombstone:

"Here lies Jane Smith, wife of Thomas Smith, marble cutter. This monument was erected by her husband as a tribute to her memory and as a sample of his work. Monuments of the same style sell for $350." Finally, there was this woman who must have been a real swinger. She's got on her husband's tombstone: "Sacred to the memory of Mr. Gerard Bates, who died August 5, 1880. His widow, age 24, who mourns as one who can be comforted, lives at 7 Elm Street, this village, and possesses every qualification of a good wife." Why not?

I pulled out these old inscriptions because as I was contemplating this first reading about Elijah, it seemed to me that he could pretty much write his own epitaph. As the story tells us, he's discouraged, the wicked Queen Jezebel is after him, all his work seems down the drain, he's at a very bad part in his life; extremely discouraged. So he treks across this desert, physically and mentally exhausted, sits beneath the broom tree, and as you heard, asks God to take his life; he's had it; enough already, I'm ready to die. His epitaph on his tombstone would probably be: "A tired and discouraged prophet."

But in the way the story has been constructed and saved and passed on to us, there is an interesting point—in the story, as we get it, God does not summon Elijah to a life hereafter as he requested, but rather to engagement in this life right now, after he has recovered. And so I suddenly began to see Elijah in a new light, as a paradigm of people like that, who have reached the bottom, who are discouraged and hurting; and if they just sit beneath the broom tree and give it time, they're going to be invited back to life in a new way, a way of wisdom.

Two extreme people came to mind as examples of this. One just a few months ago. You read in the paper of Sister Sourire. Sister Sourire was a nickname, French for "Sister Smiles" because she was always happy and smiling. She sat under her broom tree with not too good results. Some of you here are old enough to remember her as the Dominican sister years ago who made worldwide fame when it was unusual, as Sr. Dominique, the sister who sang that song "Dominique." She got a hit record out of it, and she even appeared on the *Ed Sullivan Show*, those of you who can remember that; and got a world-wide electronic audience. And she cut records and was very famous.

Well, after the seven-day wonders—you know, seven days do pass by and you're no longer a wonder—she eventually left the convent and became simply Jeanine Deckers. And then, according to the very brief report I read in the *Times* a few weeks ago, this is what happened to her: "When government spending cuts had forced the closing of a children's home that she and her companion ran, they died of an overdose of sedatives." When she sat beneath the broom tree, and, like Elijah, was in despair, her way out was to take her own life. The smiling nun smiles no longer.

I could not help contrast her to a predecessor of centuries before—Augustine of Hippo—in Africa. Augustine is at a point in his life when everything has bottomed out. He's a famous philosopher, rhetorician; but now he's getting shaky about his pagan religion. He has doubts. His relationships—with his illegitimate child, with the woman he lives with—are breaking up. He's depressed. To throw him into further despair, he's just received news that two Roman soldiers had converted to the Christian faith. Here these ignorant soldiers found something and they're happy, and he, the great intellect, is just in a terribly depressed state. As he says in his autobiography, he just went into his garden and just sat under *his* broom tree, and great man that he was, he put his head in his hands and he simply wept. As he said, he heard a voice saying, "Take and read, take and read," on the other side of the garden fence. So he went into the house and picked up the Bible, and in his own words in his autobiography he says, "I seized, opened, and in silence read that section on which my eyes first fell: 'Not in rioting and drunkenness, not in chambering and wantonness, not in strife and envying, but put on the Lord Jesus Christ and make not provision for the flesh and concupiscence.' No further would I read, nor needed I, for instantly at the end of the sentence, by a light, as it were, of serenity infused into my heart, all the darkness of doubt vanished away." So under his broom tree, he found a new direction in life.

And I think this kind of Elijah story is relevant today because we have people, people here, people all over, who are sitting beneath their broom trees. They have suffered loss—the loss of a spouse through divorce. And no matter how you slice it, divorce is lousy, as anybody knows who's been through it. On the persons, on the kids—it's not the greatest thing in the world. Loss through death—all of a sudden you're a widow or a widower. Or there's a sickness, or there's a grief; or there's a disappointment or profound hurt from your children; or from your parents, as the case may be. Or maybe there are things that you've been struggling with for years—addiction, drunkenness, alcoholism, whatever. And yet the story comes along and invites us, like Elijah, to enter life and engage it once more.

So it seems to me that there are three lessons that I pick up from this Elijah story. The first lesson is to remember. You see that is the reason that you and I gather as a church each weekend, weekend after weekend after weekend, for so many years, and hear the same old stories about Jesus and Moses and Elijah and Daniel, and all that. The point is precisely to remember. We have to keep rereading and remembering our stories so that we can be re-membered, joined to one another, and realize that someone's been there before us. And if we hear the Elijah story, and we're at our broom tree in despair, the story may encourage us that there's another way.

We hear the story of Jesus nailed to *his* tree in darkness and blackness and despair; and the resurrection gives us new hope. So the first thing we do is we re-read, and we re-listen to, and we remember the ancient stories—of the heroes and the heroines of our tradition. And that gives us a sense of direction and helps us to say "yes" to the re-invitation to engage life in a different, wiser way. That's the first thing I think this story tells us.

I think the second message is "to be still." Elijah ran and ran and ran and finally, exhausted in mind and body, sat beneath

the broom tree; and in that stillness he had a chance to regroup
and recover, and listen to the Lord. There's a lovely poem by
Grace Noel Crowell entitled "For One Who Is Tired." It goes
like this:

> Dear child, God does not say,
> "Today, be strong."
> He knows your strength is spent,
> He knows how long the road has been;
> How weary you have grown.
> For he who walked the earthly roads alone,
> Each bogging lowland and each rugged hill,
> Can understand, and so he says, "Be still
> And know that I am God." The hour is late
> And you must rest awhile; and you must wait
> Until life's empty reservoirs fill up
> As slow rains fill an empty, upturned cup.
> Hold up your cup, dear child, for God to fill.
> He only asks today that you be still.

That's a lovely metaphor. You can picture the metaphor. It's
starting to rain after a dry period, one or two drops, and you
turn your cup upside-down; and gradually, drop by drop, it
begins to fill again. Those of you who are hurting, grieving, in
sorrow, or just struggling with something, the story says maybe you need just to sit awhile and rest, and turn your cup upside-down to God; and little by little, let your dry reservoir fill
up again. *Be still.* Stop trying to control it. Be still.

And thirdly, I think, the message of Elijah is to pray for
those who are under the broom tree—yourselves, or people
that you know. Certainly the people in this world. The husband and wife who were killed the other day on 44th Street in
New York, casually, by a mugger. The people in Africa—
Indians, blacks, and whites, who are violent and killing one
another. Spouses who are destroying each other's lives. People
who are depressed because they are sick. People who are just
sad and people who are hurting. There are all kinds of people

sitting under the broom tree, wanting to write their epitaphs, and we have to pray for them. And maybe this morning, we who are at this liturgy, when in your name I lift up the paten and the chalice, you might mention someone by name in your heart and mean, "I'm laying this person's name on this paten and in this chalice and lifting it up to God because I know they're under the broom tree, and I know they they need my prayers."

So the story of Elijah is important. We've been there through the desert. We're being chased by wicked people and wicked Queen Jezebels. We're tired and weary of the same old struggle, the same old problem, and we're asking God to end it all.

But the story says, "Remember Elijah. He listened to the invitation of the Lord. Be still so you can hear God calling you anew to newness of life, and pray for those who are under the broom tree with you so that together, anew, with a different dimension in your life, you indeed may hear the voice of God."

13

+

Shadows: Father's Day

Luke 7:36–50

This is probably one of the few days this season that I can share a reflection on shadows.*

As we all know, shadows can be fun and they can be frightening. I think, as children, most of us marveled at the shadows that our bodies cast, especially in the early morning and late afternoon. Which one of us has not been tempted, and often has done, a little dance to see our shadows twirling? Or using our hands to make all kinds of pictures and shadow animals on the wall? I remember always being fascinated as a kid, marveling at how the shadows of the car followed the car wherever it went.

Of course, there's another side to shadows. There's an uncertainty about people who come out of the shadows because they are back-lit by the sun. And children can imagine many things, and not all of them very good about the shadows that play in their bedrooms when they're trying to sleep at night.

All of today's readings are about coming to terms with the frightening side of shadows.** They feature three people who did just that: King David, with his murderous adultery; Paul,

---

*A few of the ideas expressed in this homily were first inspired by material published in *Celebration: A Creative Worship Service*. The homily was given during an unusually rainy period, so there had been little sunshine.
**2 Samuel 12:7–10; Galatians 2:16; Luke 7:36–50—all for the eleventh Sunday in ordinary time. It also happened to be Father's Day.

who persecuted the church of Christ; and this unknown woman. Three genuine sinners who overcame the shadows, the shadows of the past, and learned to bask in the sun of God's forgiveness.

Now if we might identify the shadows, in our own cases, as something that we're not especially proud of, that we have done in the past; and if we identify the sun as God, then it is interesting to notice that the only time when we see our full shadow is when we turn our backs to the sun. Or to press the image to conclusion, the only time that we are overwhelmed by our sinful past is when our backs are turned to God.

When one learns to turn and face the sun, the shadow does not disappear, but it is no longer an issue. It is behind us. Our past will always be there, but when we turn to God, God helps us put the past behind us. As the sun rises in the sky, the shadows decrease in size. And as more and more we recognize that God is all-forgiving, then the shadow of our past begins to fall into place.

Of course, on the other hand, it's our experience that there are people who either hesitate or who refuse to turn to God. And you know what happens. Then their guilt moves very quickly into shame. Guilt says, "I have made a mistake." Shame says, "I am a mistake." God says that making a mistake is not the same as being a mistake. Regardless of how sinful we have been or are, we remain sons and daughters of a God who loves us, made eternally to God's image and likeness.

But there are some who, indeed, don't know this message. They haven't heard the story of David, and they haven't heard the story of Paul, and they haven't heard the story of this unnamed woman. And because they have neither heard nor seen the story they feel that their only alternative is to embrace the shadow, which, of course, will devour them. We see this among some of our young people.

One of the large issues that is attracting the attention of the psychologists, and even particularly the state police, as you may have read in the papers, is satanism among the kids. Finding the secret stars, mutilated animals, fearful things in cemeteries. It seems to have caught a lot of kids, a lot of teenagers, all across the country.

Recently they had a big meeting in New York like those held in Trenton, New Jersey. Psychologists, psychiatrists, student counselors, and state police had a discussion on this issue of Satanism among the teenagers, and younger. One of the consultants is a priest-psychologist, Father James LeBar. He had some interesting things to say and I'd like to quote a few of his sentences. He says that Satanism is an aberrational biblical cult, and he continues: "So many young people have grown up in split families with no sense of belonging. These kids have no personal faith, no community faith, and so at some point in their lives they start to search for some meaning; but by the time they get to be teenagers they have formed their own sub-culture and listened to heavy metal music."

And they then move into the shadow because no one has shown them the light. They become preoccupied with darkness, but you know, as the metaphor says, the only time you see your full shadow is when you have your back to the sun. And they don't even know that the sun is shining, or that there's a God who incredibly loves them. Or they don't even know about the stories of saints, past and present, who have come out of the shadows and have put the past behind them, and have embraced the Lord. And that's something that we can share as a faith community.

The reason that you and I are here—although individually our past may be checkered, and individually we all cast our shadows one way or another, and even individually our faith may be weak—is community faith. I like what Father LeBar said. He said, "These kids have no personal faith, no community faith." And community faith is incredibly important.

And often I could not survive, myself, when my faith gets weak and I have my own difficulties unless I have the faith of this community. And I suspect the same with you—that in our individual struggles we're weak, but the sum total, the synergism, if you will, of the people in this faith community, in varying degrees of belief and unbelief and struggle, adds up to more than the sum total of the individuals, and sustains us.

And you and I have come here and heard the ancient stories of David, who indeed did some terrible things, like adultery and murder. So do we have that on our hands? And Paul, who was a zealot for wrong causes, do we have that on our hands? But all of them refused to embrace the shadow and they turned to the Lord Jesus. And this is what we do by being here. We provide our young people an alternative to Satanism. We provide them the sun to the shadow.

There's another dimension here. These readings are very simple, and yet they're profound. The simple part was that all of these people—David, Paul, and this unknown woman— recognized the shadow and they turned to the light, Jesus. The profound part was they did not let their past get them down and wallow in it. They did something. David became an ancestor of a great lineage from which the savior came. And the murderous Saul went out and lived and preached the word of God. And we can hardly believe that this woman went back and said, "Now my sins are forgiven, I can sit home and knit." She went out and proclaimed to the village, "I met someone who gave light to my darkened life and I want to share that with you."

Because it's Father's Day, there is, I think, an extra dimension to our Scripture readings and our worship today. I think that uniquely, above all others, fathers set the tone as to where light and darkness are. I think, above all others, fathers tell their sons and daughters by word and action that there is a sun that they can turn to. That they don't have to wallow in their shadows, if they just do a turnabout. There's a God who loves them. Especially fathers who know what forgiveness is.

To borrow a cliché from all those bumper stickers, "If fathers set the tone, forgiven fathers do it better." Fathers who themselves know forgiveness. They're better able to show their children what it means. And after all, the fact is, psychologically and spiritually, that unconsciously we all take our first impressions of God from our own fathers because one of the first prayers we learn is "Our Father who art in heaven," and the first overlay of that main Father is the father that we know; the only fatherly identity that we know.

And that's why fathers are important. They set up the pattern for their children. Not to embrace the shadow, no matter how many terrible deeds they've done, but to turn to God. Every father is a prodigal father, having the possibility of taking a prodigal son and daughter and saying, "Look, you've disgraced us. You've been into all kinds of terrible things. You've embarrassed us to death. You've hurt our family name. But our arms are open." And once they learn that from daddy, God the Father is an easy jump.

Some of you remember "Soapy" Williams, the late governor of Michigan. I heard him tell this story once, about part of his family life. He was watching his son struggling to carry heavy rocks across the lawn. He was making some kind of a fort or foundation, or whatever. And Soapy called across to his son and he said, "Son, why don't you call upon all your resources?" And the son protested, "But Dad, I am." And his father said, "But you haven't asked me to help you." I think that's where fathers are important. They're a resource. They point to God, and they know their own shadow side, but they have refused to embrace it. And all you fathers who are here today are witnesses to that.

The conclusion to this reflection is a gift. It is our custom on Mother's and Father's Day to give a little gift after the homily, and so today we have a gift for the fathers. The gift that we have is a little lapel pin. It's in the shape of a fish that has a cross in it.

Some of you may recollect that the fish was the first sign of being a Christian because when you take in Greek the letters of the word fish, *ichthus*, they stand also for "Jesus Christ, Son of God, Savior." And when the Christians were being persecuted, and they wanted secretly to identify themselves to other Christians, so they wouldn't get caught, they would use their toe of their sandal or a stick and would make a little shape of a fish in the sand as they were talking casually. It was a form of secret identification of Christians.

So we'd like to give this sign to the fathers because, as I said, uniquely, I think, they are signs of Jesus. I think they're the secret sign of what forgiveness is about. I think they are the sign of the sun, as opposed to the shadow. I think that fathers who wear this give notice that "I belive in Jesus. I'm not only a father, I'm a forgiven father, and I'm going to try to forgive my children."

So that's the gift of Scripture to us. And this is our gift to you.

14

+

What Are We To Do?

Luke 3:1–19

The gospel focuses on John the Baptist. John the Baptist is called the precursor, the one who runs before to prepare the way. This was a very common Oriental custom and Mid Eastern custom. When the local potentate was going around visiting his domains, such as they were, the precursors went ahead and cleared the roads and literally straightened out all the rough paths.

If you want an idea of John the Baptist, there were thousands of them when Gorbachev came to New York. They were playing John the Baptist roles—straightening out the streets, keeping the traffic away, causing the "Gorby Gridlock"—that sort of thing. But that's exactly what they were doing. A potentate was coming—a leader of state—and they prepared the way for that.

One of the interesting things in the Scripture here that you can read easily between the lines is this: one of the rough ways for a lot of people is the past. People who have done things that were minor to major. People like any one of us here who can look back over our shoulder and see some of the less than gracious things we've either done or we've said. Things that have hurt people, and in some instances, things that were enormously evil. Spouses betrayed. Deaths in the family. Dishonesty. Embezzlement. Fraud and lying. Murder. Drugs. Addictions. The catalog is as endless as there are people. For you and for me, they're there.

So for some people, the past is an enormously rough way. They turn and they dwell on it, and they do not make progress because they're always looking back. And so when these people with a past came to John, they asked him that question that was repeated several times in the gospel: "What are we to do? What ought we to do?"—the people, the tax collectors, the soldiers. But you noticed John's answer. Not in any instance did John advise them to review or dwell on the past. John's idea was that "Look, here you are, here and now, asking for baptism, renewal, something in the future to expect, a better life." And so John answers them not in the past—he answers them in the future.

So to the tax collectors: "From now on, I'm not caring what you did in the past, whatever evil, and how much you've hurt people; but from now on, in the future, here's what to do. Don't extort more than what you're supposed to collect." And to the soldiers, no matter how much brutality and pillage and rape they had done in the past: "You're asking me 'what are we to do?' Look to the future. Do not bully people and do not hurt others."

I was reminded of that because I came across a little saying the other day from a Dr. Loomis who wrote an article. He was near the end of his own life and he wanted to leave some kind of wisdom from his twenty-five years of practice. What inspired him was a line from George Eliot, a line that says, "It's but little good you'll do watering last year's crops."

And Dr. Loomis wrote this. He said, "Watering last year's crops is exactly what I have seen hundreds of my patients doing in the past twenty-years. Watering with freely flowing tears things of the irrevocable past. Not the bittersweet memories of loved ones, which I can understand, but things done which should not have been done, and things left undone which should have been done. Moaning over what cannot be helped is a confession of selfishness and cowardice. The best way to break this morbid circle, to snap out of it, is to stop thinking about yourself and to start thinking about others. You can lighten your load by doing something for someone else. By the simple act of doing an outward, unselfish act today you can make the past recede, and the present and future will take on their true perspective. As a doctor, I have seen it tried many, many times, and nearly always it has been a far more successful prescription than any I could have ordered at the drugstore."

I think we find this in the gospel. What are we to do? And I think if John were here he would say, "Look, all of us here right now are sitting in this building. Everyone of us has a past—mild, benign, comfortable, indifferent, horrendous, or sinful." John would say, "But the thing you want to look at is this: you're here, aren't you? You're sitting here in order to worship God and to hear the good news and break bread together as a community of faith. Whatever has been in the past—hurt or death, or divorce, you name it—it's the past."

And if you've come here to say, "Lord, God, what ought we to do?", the Lord God will look at you and say, "Well, the first thing, you are here, and that's a plus." And you can't undo the past, and what can we say about that? But if you really believe in the future, if you believe in the expectation, and the coming of Christ, what Advent is all about, then the only way to live is to start today to do the good deed. Because once you move out of yourself, and once you stop looking over your shoulder, that's the only way that you can grow. Let the past bury the past. There are a lot of things you and I have not liked seeing in the paper—some things we're ashamed of. Okay, but it's gone.

But the prophet would say, "If you're asking me what you want to do, there's the future. God has allotted you so many days—use them for other people. It doesn't have to be a magnificent gesture; it just has to be an everyday kindness."

I was reminded of that because in doing a little Christmas shopping, I came across a Chris Williamson album. (Some of you may or may not know her name; she's a songwriter and recording artist.) And I was reading the jacket of her Christmas album and I didn't want to read all of it, but something caught my eye. She was just telling the story of when she was a little girl and lived in Wisconsin, out in the wild boondocks there in a little place called Moonlight Ranch. It's very cold there—if you've been out in that part of the Midwest, you have an idea of thirty-foot snows and all that sort of thing.

She was telling about near Christmas time when they were getting ready, and the great treat was to put the angel on the top of the tree. She was sitting in the kitchen for her annual haircut. It's a small cabin and she's sitting there and there's newspaper on the floor and her mother's cutting her hair to shoulder length. Here's the way she described it. She says, "It was a great honor in our family to be chosen to place the Christmas angel on the very tip of the tree. Dad would hold the chosen child high in the air and the angel would slip over the tip until it shone high above the room. That Christmas, as the afternoon gave way to gradual darkness, Mom cut my hair. My long braids had been shorn to shoulder length and the hair was all around me on the floor. I remember feeling sort of small as I sat there on my hard chair in the kitchen. Dad came in out of the frosty cold with an armload of stove wood. He put it in the wooden box beside the stove and looked over at me, sitting so pensively on my chair. He knelt down beside me and picked up all the hair, newly shorn from my head. The next thing I knew he was calling us to the front room where the Christmas tree stood in all of its shining splendor. I watched him as he carefully placed bits of my brown hair on the tree beside the tinsel and the glittering glass balls. He turned and smiled sweetly down at me and said, 'This year we will have real angel hair on the tree.' "

It's as simple as something like that, isn't it? The good deed, the kindness. It was St. Paul who said that charity overcomes a multitude of sins. And charity in the future overcomes the mistakes and the sadnesses and the necessary losses of the past.

So picture yourself in line. The people—"What are we to

do?" The soldiers—"What ought we to do?" And you and I—"What ought we to do?" John would say, "Don't look at the past. It's gone. If you look for the expectation of Christ in your heart, you'll see a road ahead paved by good deeds."

You can't obliterate the past. But you can make it recede. You can learn to live with the scars. You can learn to live with the disappointment that your children have given you, the hurt that they've given you. Or a former spouse or whatever. You can learn to live with that—if only you get out of yourself and do the good deed, and in turn, become John the Baptist and pave the way for others so that they, too, may have the opportunity to look into the face of the messiah.

15

✛

Designer Worth
Matthew 6:25–34

Perhaps I'd better introduce these remarks with a little thing I've got here from *Reader's Digest*, and it says, "Real life is very different from soap opera life. For example, in real life you go to fewer than four parties a week; you have to look up phone numbers; your great-grandmother looks her age; you have a priest who falls asleep while hearing your confession; Monopoly is a game and not a way of life; you and your spouse probably do not fit into the bathtub at the same time; and the odds are that the only time you were ever in a home worth more than a million dollars was when you paid two dollars a head for the tour."

And I introduce that because the readings today are kind of intriguing. In the first reading, as you may have noticed, the eleven apostles were there. It was after the death and resurrection of Jesus, and they were anxious to fill up the number to twelve—twelve being a kind of mystical representation of completeness; and you have to sense the anxiety. The anxiety not just that there should be twelve apostles, but rather the anxiety revealed by the term that they used, that we should have a full toll of witnesses—that was uppermost in their minds. Witnesses to what? Why were they anxious about that?

Well, they felt that if witnesses were deficient, then the pagan world would go abounding and never hear the word, and in the gospel, Jesus was insistent: "Look, I have given you the word, the word of God; that God is love, that God loves you intimately." And it was so important, that above the shout of the world, this message would get through. And if you had not enough witnesses, then the whole mission of Jesus would collapse. So basically, they had to vote in someone else, and the vote was concerned with the need, as I said, that the living word, the word that bespoke a value system, would at least be heard. Whether people acted on it or not is another story.

So with these texts in mind—the Acts of the Apostles and the gospel of John—let me move into two modern texts to translate that: one, the *New York Times*, and the other, an issue of *Forbes* Magazine.

A while back, the *New York Times*, on the inside page, had a headline, "Painting the Lilies: Cosmetics for Babies," and the opening paragraph says, "Cosmetic companies are going after a new market, young children. The industry is courting the upscale cradle set with fragrances, soaps and mousse shampoos, sun blocks (whatever they are), and even a scent for those born yesterday." These scents cost thirty dollars for 3.3 ounces. They have a soap called Gregory for baby boys, which is fifteen-fifty for 0.85 ounces. They are marketing these things for young children who are one to three years old. Advertisements show a youngster in a white suit leaning against a pint-sized Mercedes convertible.

Who buys all of this? A man named Allen Moltses, a marketing consultant for the cosmetic industry, says, and I quote: "It seems to be for guilty yuppie parents who work all the time and want to smother their children with little goodies." Psychologists and psychiatrists such as Dr. Lee Salk, a pediatric psychiatrist, are very upset about this sort of thing. He says, "I feel it's a negative thing, these cosmetics for infants, in the same way that beauty contests among children are clearly destructive. Vanity has its place later on when people have developed values." Well, of course, there's the point. The point is that they are selling a value system.

Why would you need cosmetics or perfume for newborn babies? Newborn babies and infants have a marvelous natural smell. They always smell good, except at diaper time. But they do. You will notice everyone loves to cuddle them. They just have that natural aura. And why you would want to deodorize and delouse the poor little infants so early and then re-scent him or her at thirty bucks a throw? But you see the message.

The message of all advertising is, you are defective. That's the bottom line. If you weren't defective, you wouldn't need our products; but somehow, somewhat, even hiddenly, you may look the picture of health and everything else, but even though you cleared up the underarm stains, there may still be odors that you are unaware of that are prostrating people around the table. So therefore you are defective, and you are only worth something if you buy an external product at a large cost and apply it to yourself.

Now that may seem rather frivolous, but behind that is a theological question, believe it or not, that deals with the Scripture because the witness that Jesus wants has a different message that says you are fundamentally valuable just by "being." The old catechism had a phrase that said, "you are made in the image and likeness of God," but as soon as you are devoid and robbed of that concept, then the only other thing is to go and acquire worth; and in a consumer society such as America, acquiring worth means consuming and purchasing.

That brings us to our second text, in *Forbes* magazine. The article is called, "What Is Perfume But Water and a Bit of Essence?" It highlights Pierre Cardin, who promoted the designer label craze. Everybody knows, intellectually, that the very identical item, whether it is jeans or frying pans, will cost a couple of dollars more just by the application of a designer label, although it is the identical product.

So even though, intellectually, we know that, we buy designer things and products and clothes; and so you have to ask yourself why. Why do we pay so much? According to this article, Pierre Cardin alone gets two billion dollars a year just by letting someone sew two words on frying pans or underwear or clothes or whatever, and you have to wonder what is behind that.

So they asked Bornstein, the historian down in Washington, who has written several marvelous books, and he has some insightful comments that, again, we can put into a scriptural context. He said once upon a time people thought of themselves in ethnic, political, and religious terms. For example: I am a Midwestern Republican Presbyterian, or I am a Southern Baptist Democrat, or I am of Scottish-Irish descent, and so on.

People still do that, but superimposed on the older order is a sense of identity born of a consumer society. Therefore, I am a white-wine-drinking, Rolex-watch-wearing, Volvo driver. Now as soon as I say that, I am sure there are about three of you in here with Rolexes on, rolling down your sleeves, and walking home and not taking your Volvo.

But you see what's behind that. He says the tastes have gone beyond boundaries. He says a consumer community consists of people who have a feeling of shared well-being, shared risks, common interests, and common concerns that come from consuming the same kind of objects. Porsche drivers, *Forbes* readers, Gucci loafer wearers—these are just many of the thousands of consumption communities. The nice thing about consumption communities is that they are democratic—anybody can join. You don't have to have family connections, or diplomas from the right school, or drink Chivas Regal, or drive a Mercedes or collect art. All you need is lots of money.

The designer label, he says, is the application of the concept of celebrity to the consumption community. That is, the designer label designates a community of consumers on whom some of the celebrity name rubs off, and so it is that underwear by Jockey or Hanes is just underwear, but underwear by Pierre Cardin or Percy Ellis is a personal statement: "I am an avant-garde fellow like Pierre. I am proud to associate with like-minded people, and I don't mind paying extra for the privilege."

Well, there it is. The triumph of a consumer society that says you are only worth something if you have someone else's name. The deep theology (which is not thought through, of course) behind things like that is what I said before. You have no worth but what is conferred. You see the logical extension in abortion. The child has no worth unless the mother puts thumbs up or thumbs down and says, "Yes, you have worth," or "No, you don't have worth."

You see another extension of that when you read these poignant stories of the kids who are making three or four or five hundred dollars a day running drugs, and you say, "Why did you drop out of school and why are you running drugs?" "Because of all that money, man. You can buy the right car and wear the right watches and have the right designer clothes, and therefore 'I am somebody.' " In a society that spends billions of dollars to tell you that you're nobody unless you consume, the drug running kids are prime examples of that; and of course television provides society's images of what it means to be somebody: the lives of the rich and famous.

But what happens, of course, is the designer label brings its own tyrannies. Parents and teachers tell me that sometimes their children will not go to school unless they have the proper designer clothes. One woman told me that yesterday, when I preached this at the five-o'clock Mass. She said, "Yes, the parents took out one of the kids in my high school and are sending her to a parochial school because in my high school they even have designer book covers; and if you just didn't have the right designer label, you were nothing."

Comedian Mort Sahl said it well years ago. He said, "Ask a Californian who he is and he points to his car." Well, now that's true of all fifty states. We are identified by what we have, and the insidiousness, if you will, of the designer label culture (as I say, look behind it) is a theological horror. And you can see why in the context of the Scripture—Jesus and followers are anxious for a full toll of witnesses, witnesses who say, "But there is another measurement of humankind: you are valuable because you are you. Even though you don't live in the right house or the right neighborhood or have the right address, you are still valuable."

That helps us to be empathetic for the downtrodden and the homeless and those who have far less to eat then we do. That makes going to school not just a means to get more money so that you can die of overconsumption. And, of course, everything that you purchase, you realize, is a separatist item. Every new thing separates human beings. Every additional room in the house puts space between people. Every additional activity takes you away from the family meal, so that you hardly sit around the table and talk. Every designer label, especially that one you insist on, that one you are nobody without, cuts down on your image as made to the image and likeness of God, and makes you always anxious to purchase your value and sell yourself to get attention.

So the Christian witness says this: you are as good as much as you recognize that you are a son or daughter of God; you are as good as the deeds you do. In Catholic theology we call this corporal and spiritual works of mercy. If you want to know your inner worth, just answer these questions: "When I was hungry, did you give me to eat? When I was thirsty, did you give me to drink? When I was in prison, did you visit me?" That's the only measurement Jesus ever gave for getting into heaven, for separating the sheep and goats.

So the Scripture kind of puts things into context; its meaning isn't a ranting and raving against retail people like Cardin and Yves St. Laurent and all those; rather the gospel offers us a reflection; it gives us a perspective. And you can tell the gospel has hit home when, for example, you come to realize that you have to have designer clothes, or at least realize they have become so important that they become necessary. And when you scream to your neighbor or to your parents that you simply cannot go here or there without them, then you know that deep down underneath you have fallen prey to a terrible situation that will forever measure you in terms of quantity and quality.

Are you a loving person? Are you a moral person? Are you

virtuous? Do you keep your word? Can we trust you? Can you make commitments and honor them? Can you say "I'm sorry"? Can you say "I love you"? Can you express your feelings? Can you show love?

Think of the marvelous people who wouldn't even think of wearing designer clothes—maybe a Mother Teresa—but she's not popular in that set, you see. So the message of the Acts of the Apostles here is this: "Look, it's necessary to have a full toll of witnesses, and that includes people like you, you and me, who find we can buy all of these things. That's great, except we have to know what we're doing; and we also have to know where the line gets crossed when we start talking and thinking in terms of labels. Then we know we have become a victim and not a witness."

Remember that Jesus said, in effect: "Look, I've given my word to you and you've got to go out there," and remember that he prayed so beautifully; "Almighty Father, I do not ask you to take the people out of the world [no, that's where we live, that's where we belong], but I ask you to protect them from the evil one." And the evil one is the evilness of equating *you* with the things you own. If you do that, when you become ugly through sickness, and when you are lying putrid on your deathbed, nobody will want to hug you. When these "things" can't matter anymore because you are depressed or emotionally upset, you will still want to know you are worth something. But if you don't equate yourself with what you own and then you lose all your "things" through a crash in the market, you won't jump off the bridge, because you will know you are more than your job.

Last week I went back to a little graduation party at Boston College. And when I was up there I picked up the *Boston Globe* and read, to my sadness, that another kid up at M.I.T. jumped off the thirteenth story of a building and killed himself. Out of a possible 4.0, a perfect score, he was a student who got 3.96. He was a genius, but he still felt inadequate. And then, of course, you have all the outpourings in the editorials. Well, he was the thirteenth one to commit suicide since this school year began.

The editorials talk about the unrelenting move for technical excellence and for achievement. They point to the fact that these hyper schools like M.I.T. are scientifically probably the best in the world. That's all important, but the real issue is whether we make room for the humanness of the student. The important thing is whether we say, "Hey, if you are not perfect we still love you. Your worth is not tied up in getting the best marks so that the greatest engineering corporation in the world will pick you up and start you out at $50,000 a year. Even if you don't get that job, *you* are *who* you are, the very image and likeness of God. And God loves you deeply."

The word of God that Jesus speaks is the word that he knows from his ancestral Scriptures. He would quote to us maybe Isaiah, where God says to the people, "Can a mother forget the child of her womb? Of course not, but even if she should, I will not forget you, my people." Or through Jeremiah he says, "Behold, I love you with an everlasting love." Or the night before he dies, Jesus himself said, "Look, I no longer call you servants, but I call you friends."

If you could spend some time on getting to know that you're a friend of Jesus, that God loves you so deeply, and that God is closer to you than you are to yourself, then you would not have to over-worry about your clothes or your wristwatch or your car, or the fact that you didn't make the dean's list. We just have to know that we are who we are, that's what St. Paul said, writing from prison just before he died; and maybe we might close with those words. Looking back over his hectic life, he says, "By the grace of God I am what I am; and the grace of Jesus Christ has not been void in me."

That's who you are—a person graced by Christ forever, an image of God forever. Nobody can take that from you and nobody can sew it onto you. By the grace of Christ, you are who you are.

16

✝

Radical Saints

Matthew 19:16–22; Mark 10:17–22

We know, of course, the rest of this gospel story. The young man could not follow Jesus because as the gospel comments, "he had many possessions." And although he was a good person, he could not break away from them.

Our understanding of what the gospel means, of course, is that he was called to a more profound life of discipleship, good as he was, and he found it difficult to answer that call. Those who do answer the call are the ones that we term as "saints."

We've recently been celebrating an array of very popular saints in our liturgical calendar. We've been celebrating the feast of Vincent de Paul, for example; the big Saint, Saint Teresa of Avila, the Spanish mystic and doctor of the church; the little Saint Therese, remember, the Little Flower; Saint Francis of Assisi, who is probably the most popular saint in all the Christendom and even among nonbelievers.

The difficulty with the saints for us, however, is twofold. One, I think we've gotten so used to them—particularly those of us who might come from pre-modern churches when you had a lot of statues around, and you had your Bible histories and books, and lives of the saints. And so we became so familiar that we have taken them for granted. But perhaps even worse than that, what we have done with our saints is that we have sentimentalized them; and that's probably the worst service we could do to them.

I suspect if we asked some of you your image of, let's say, the two most popular saints, Francis of Assisi and the Little Flower, the images would be pretty clear and predictable. He'd be wearing this kind of Franciscan cloth with the rope around his waist; he'd have sandals on his feet; he'd have his large, round tonsure, and he would be out giving a sermon to the birds. Therese would be dressed in her Carmelite outfit as we remember the statues; she would have a cross on her arm filled with roses and she would be dropping down rosebuds from heaven onto the people on earth.

The difficulty about that is when we confine them to those images we take away their real power. The fact is that what made these two people (or any saint) saints was their radical-ness, in the original sense of the word. A radical is one who goes to the root of things, that's where we get it. And Therese and Francis and all the rest may not have always been right, or even been balanced, but that's not the point. The point was that there was a gospel that confronted them and in a most radical way they responded to it.

Take Francis of Assisi, for example. He was a rich man's son. He had every right to encourage his father's very lucrative cloth business. All that he cared about, as we would say today, was to party. He was known for that. And yet this young man not out of his teens had a crisis. He went off to war thinking it would be fun and games all the way. But he wound up in pris-on, when he had kind of a crisis in his life, and a breakdown. When he forced himself to embrace a leper, he began to look at the gospel anew—especially passages like "Leave all things and follow me" or this gospel of Mark that he read. He read the words "Leave all things and come follow me," and there was only one thing left—Francis decided to act. He acted so far that he even, like most saints, did a most radical thing—that fa-mous scene where he stood in the village square, you remember, and took off all his clothes and walked away stark naked; his symbol of putting aside all the wealth and privilege that his parents had in store for him, because he wanted to follow Jesus. Now, if you think that's easy, probably the best thing is to transfer that scene to today.

Francis becomes a young man who lives in a wealthy suburb, his parents with lots of money. He came from that kind of background, with all the privilege he could expect. A car at graduation, college taken care of, a big house, a good future assured for him. Those of you who are parents here, just think of what it would mean for your nineteen-year-old son to tell you that he's heard a call, and through a crisis in his life, he has listened to the gospel, and like this young man, he has decided to give up all this and go and work among the poor. And to be sure that you understood what he was saying, and how sincere he was, he rejected your car and the house and your designer clothes, and put on simple jeans and a sweatshirt, and off he went down to Appalachia to minister to the poor people there. Just think of that, now. Appreciate how radical this is. My guess is that most parents would send him to a behavioral psychologist to have his behavior modified. Think of what this meant. And this is what the idea of sainthood means; this idea of a kind of radical statement to say "yes" to the gospel; to go to the root of what Jesus wanted.

Some of you may have heard of Sister Emmanuel Chinquin. She literally lives in the garbage dumps outside of Cairo, in Egypt, where the poor people live. And that's where they not only live, but when people throw their garbage, they get their food and clothes from whatever can be gotten from that garbage. It's a dark and dangerous place. Even the police won't go there. And yet Sister Emmanuel is there. And you may also have heard of the fruits of her work. There's a clinic, a school, houses, and their precious compost factory.

Sister Emmanuel is eighty years old. Listen to two things that she said about all this. She said, "In the slum we love each other and we share with each other. In my poor slum we laugh much. And, of course, in the big modern cities the people don't even know each other. You can change people's lives if you first affirm their lives by living as they do. Of course, the rag pickers and garbage collectors are despised, and that's the reason I came here: to share their lives night and day, to prove to them that they're human beings and that they're sons and daughters of God." Sister Emmanuel does not consider herself a saint, but she is, in the sense that she has made a radical, root response to the gospel of Jesus Christ; watched him go out to the highways and byways and gather in the disenfranchised; and she has done that.

If you want to come closer to home, let me share a letter that we received not long ago. As you know, we have a tithing committee. We tithe 10 percent of our gross income that we get from you each year. One-third goes to international needs, one-third to national, and one-third to local. The tithing committee scans all these things to try to give to the best possible need. Well, we had a little extra reason to reach out to Alaska this time, to the missions up there, because Jimmy Gallagher, the son of members of our community, has taken a year out of his young life to give to the Jesuit Volunteer Corps. They go to the worst parts of the world to give a year of their talent and lives to help these people.

And so, in the midst of a very fine career, of a very bright and intelligent boy who's going to go far, he's heard the gospel and decided to take out a year of his life and do something for somebody. So we sent a third of our tithing, some $30,000, up to Bean's Cafe. Bean's Cafe is not a nightclub; it's just what they call their little hovel and mission where these poor people live. So Jim wrote a letter and he says: "Dear Friends: Whoever would have thought that a two-page summary of my decision to become a Jesuit Volunteer would net a whopping cash donation for Bean's Cafe? I must say it's not a bad deal. As we are more than a little isolated, Alaskans tend to be a rather independent lot. 'Alaska for Alaskans' is the bumper sticker commonly seen throughout the state. Similarly, our social service system is a self-contained network. Donations of food, time, and money are given generously, and the results of this good will are readily discernible within the community. This is to give you some idea of how unique your gift is: the unconditionality of your donation is inspiring. To think that someone outside of Alaska cares that we exist and recognizes the great need within our huge, sparsely populated state. We have only one-sixteenth of the population of New York City."

Then he makes a little personal contribution that sounds like Francis of Assisi: "As significant were the personal implications. When I chose to do a year of volunteer work with the Jesuit Volunteer Corps in Anchorage, I met with a number of reactions, not all of which were positive. This surprised and disappointed me, as some of this negative feedback came from individuals who have taken part in my Christian upbringing. That the community of St. Mary's that I grew up with cared enough to support Bean's Cafe says to me that they approve of my decision and the path that my life has taken. I take it as more than a generic blessing, but rather a care and concern for what I am doing, even after so many years away from the town where I grew up. Thank you for bringing my two worlds a little bit closer together."

So there's someone in our midst who listened to the gospel and said, "With all the privilege that I have here, I'm going to go and live among the poorest of the poor in Anchorage, Alaska."

This is what the gospel is saying. It's talking about sainthood. It doesn't mean we're perfect, or even right, as I said, or even emotionally balanced. To be a saint is to be one who listens to the gospel and asks, "In my lifetime and space how can I live out the gospel, come what may?"

Therese, the Little Flower, we also tend to sentimentalize, but you have to remember she died of TB when she was twenty-four years old. She went through bouts of depression, and particularly bouts of doubt about her faith. Her heroism is not that she hid away in a Carmelite monastery. Her heroism was that, like Jesus on the cross, when everything seemed lost and dark and bleak, she commended herself to God despite her doubts and her struggles with faith.

So you see, the saints are radical. They go right to the root of what the gospel's about: trust and love, throwing themselves into the arms of God, hoping they'll be caught; listening to Jesus' words of invitation—"Come and follow me"; and they leave all things and do precisely that.

You think of ordinary people like us. Dr. Tom Dooley, who leaves a lucrative practice to take care of the orphans in Viet Nam. Dorothy Day, who could have made big money on *The New York Times*. What drove those people to turn their backs on great advancement as the world knows it, and to give their lives in service like that?

Not all of us can leave all things, or go to the slum garbage pits of Cairo, or the depressed area of Anchorage, Alaska, but sainthood says that in our lives there are radical decisions that can be made: where we live, the type of clothes we wear, the cars we buy, the concerns in our hearts, the priorities of our lives, the relationships with one another. These are radical things that can put values of the gospel first, often at great personal cost.

So we're like that man in the gospel. We say, "I'm a good person," and indeed we are. We say, "I've kept all these commandments, Lord. What else is left?" And Jesus looks at us with love and says, "Well, I've got one more thing. You could become a saint."

Each of us has his or her own answer to that.

17

Halloween

Revelation 7:9–17

This weekend, as you know, all throughout our land we have big and little goblins and ghosts and spirits who will be patroling the streets asking for tricks or treats. And so we celebrate this kind of secular day with fun, but after that, does it say anything to us; and behind the Halloweening, are there a Christian residue and message?

I'd like to share with you what are, perhaps, some of the origins of Halloween, and accordingly, what we can do from a faith perspective to place it in our lives.

As far as we can tell, Halloween comes from the old Celtic celebrations of the end of the summer. The reason they had a feast to mark the end of summer was because it was when the spirits began to have more time to roam the land. As lore has it, the spirits come out at night. Well now that we're at the end of summer, you see, the days are shorter and the winter nights are longer and so it gives the goblins and spirits a greater time to work their habits. And so to appease such spirits who now have a longer haunting time, the pagans offered them treats so they would not be the object of their tricks.

Of course, among them as always, there were those enterprising citizens of that island who took to disguising themselves as evil spirits—number one, so they could fool the real spirits so they would leave them alone; and of course, number two, dressed up as evil spirits themselves, they could go around stealing the treats.

Well, you see, it was this kind of thing that the Christians met when they came along, and as is the custom of good Christian tradition, they baptized the pagan custom that the pagans already had in mind; that is, they sifted out what was true and they shucked off the superstitious. (As a parenthetical remark, by the way, this is where we differ from fundamentalists. A teacher told me years ago that a parent of a child in her fourth grade would not allow her little boy to participate in any Halloween kind of celebration because it was not in the Bible, and it was a pagan custom.)

But Catholic Christianity has never had trouble with that. Catholic Christianity has always said that wherever there is truth, it's truth; whether Muhammad or Buddha, or whoever speaks it. And Catholic Christianity, therefore, both recognizes and validates the truth and builds upon it.

So in this case, you had this old Celtic end of summer celebration, and Christians came along and this is what they did. They remembered, in fact, that there's a spirit world, and so maybe it was good opportunity to draw these pagans into remembering all the spirits, all the deceased. And so this pagan custom became "All Hallows Eve"—the word "hallows," as you know, means "holy," as in "hallowed be thy name." And so this was remembering all the holy ones who have gone before us.

And once that was in place—remembering all the holy ones who were deceased—then around the fourth century it was easy to introduce the Feast of All Saints, which started out as the Feast of All the Martyrs, and place it at the end of the summer right next to this remembering of the spirits. And then a few centuries later it was easy to introduce what we call the Feast of All Souls, on the next day.

And so, for Christians what came from a pagan origin was united with this incredibly beautiful concept from Jesus: I am the vine, you are the branches; or St. Paul's concept of the mystical body of Christ; which is to say that we have a great consciousness, in our tradition, that we are united with those in the past, present, and those to come.

We celebrate, for example, our Mass of Christian Burial; and in that Mass there are notes of celebration, because we say that this person has not had a period put on the end of his or her life, but they have exchanged one kind of living here for a different kind of living hereafter. And so, there's a firm Catholic belief in the afterlife, and a firm Catholic belief in an intercessory connection with all those who have gone before.

What that means is that what we have here is a secular celebration, which is fine, and we should enjoy it, which is even better, but beyond that here's what it can say to Christians: First, dressing up for Halloween—yourself, or your children, or your grandchildren, whoever—can ritually join us to the past, present, and those to come. In other words, when you (or members of your family) get dressed up in your ghostly costume, just try to remember it's a ritual way of being connected to the spirit world; a ritual way of saying that we believe in the unity of the entire human race.

Secondly, it's a way of affirming our traditional belief in the spirit world, the supernatural. We believe in angels; we believe in saints. We believe that an end is not simply put to the lives of our parents who are deceased, but there is a livingness that continues.

Thirdly, there's another interesting thing. When we don those horrible masks, which are scary (but in a certain sense they are not, because we are in control, like a parent who's reading a ghost story to a child—the child is both scared and comforted because the parent/savior is right there to keep him or her safe), it becomes a symbol that behind the horrors of the disfigurement brought on by hurt or pain or sin or sickness, or even death, behind those masks is the face of Jesus Christ. That God has the last word in Christ; that any ugliness will be made beautiful; any sin can be forgiven, and even the last enemy, death, shall give way to the life of Jesus. They can tell us that.

And finally, it seems to me, Halloween can be a little anti-

dote to our pride and our arrogance in the sense that we don't
know everything; that we live in mystery. Mystery is very uncomfortable, particularly to Americans who are raised up in a
very positivistic attitude. We want to be able to dissect and
control everything, and yet in much of our lives we don't.
There are mysteries that we live everyday, including the greatest mystery of all—the mystery of ourselves. And so dressing
up for Halloween, and moving in and out, the fun of ghosts
and skeletons and spirits, reminds us that we do live in mystery. So Halloween can have its positive Christian side.

I have some suggestions before we go trick or treating for
those who might want to think about them. Four suggestions:

One is this: Those of you who do go celebrating, or dress up
and carry on in any way for Halloween—before you go out
trick or treating, I just suggest that you gather for a moment or
two—in the dining room or wherever—and offer a prayer for
all deceased family members, friends, people of your past.
That's what Halloween is all about. It's about a ghostly
world—people who are dead, but who live; people who have
passed on—but it's our belief that they live on in Christ.

And in praying for those deceased, pray not only for the
good, but for the wicked. People who have been wicked or
horrible to you, and made a mess of your life or hurt you in
some way. That would be in the spirit of Bob Cratchit, you
know, who on Christmas Eve toasts Ebenezer Scrooge, because
if he's a real Christian, he has to even pray for the wicked. So
remember those, and remember those especially who shared
the faith with you, those who are responsible for your being in
church today; all holy people, whether they walk with us or not,
from any tradition, who are struggling for peace and justice.

So the first thing I might suggest to you to keep the Christian
motif in Halloween is just gather for prayer to remember the
spirit world, those in your family and others who have gone
on to God.

Secondly, I might suggest, to emphasize this, that you drag
out the family album; or if you have a picture or Grandmom or
Grandpop or somebody who's deceased, that you just take it

off the wall or out of the album or open it up on the coffee table; maybe just light a little candle in front of it; but some kind of emphasis to your children and your children's children that we come from a long line of people. We carry their genes, we carry their values; whatever and whoever we are, there was someone in our past—we are not disconnected atoms. And so bring out Grandmom's or Grandpop's or Aunt Susie's picture, and just put it there to remind the family that we are just a moment in a long, common journey of all humankind, to God. It might be good to make this a Halloween custom; and maybe from October 31st through November 2nd keep the picture in a special place just to remind us of where we come from.

Thirdly, I might suggest that as a part of Halloween you have your family members research their saint's name. Whose name is it that they bear? What's the history of this hero or heroine? And maybe the next time they have a birthday, they could share with the rest of the family whom they were named after and what that person says to them now.

And the final suggestion would be that all those not immediately perishable things that you might get for trick or treating—that you might come and place them in front of the altar. The church is always open, as you know. And we'll see that people who are less fortunate get a share of the goodies that you've collected.

So it's a way of saying that Halloween, which started out as a pagan custom, had a basically good thought. Those pagans were aware that they moved and lived in a world that was much larger than themselves. Christians have taken that over and celebrate those who have meant to much to us—the great saints, and those who are yet to come.

So as we go around, and as we dress up and as we make ourselves scary, just try to recollect some of these thoughts. It's a Christian feast in many ways. All Saints, All Souls, both living and dead. And we can enter into the spirit; and we can realize that indeed we are not alone. We belong to this vast company of the gone-before, yet-to-come. We are not alone; we belong to the communion of saints.

18

✝

The Cross That Shapes Us

Mark 5:25–34

Maybe we want to reflect quietly on what I think is perhaps another approach to this very interesting Marcan gospel.

What you perceive here is a very common Marcan way—or St. Mark's way—of constructing his gospel. What he does, as you see here, is to take an incident such as that involving Jairus's daughter, her father coming to ask Jesus to cure her. And as Jesus is on the way to Jairus's house, Mark sandwiches in another story about a woman who had been afflicted with hemorrhage for twelve years. And after that incident he returns to the daughter of Jairus.

But it's the woman that I would like to reflect on with you, because it is another woman who gave me a different perspective on what may have happened here.

The first thing that Mark notices is that it's been twelve years, and he also mentions "she had suffered much." Imagine twelve years with a problem—or as we would express it today—"twelve years carrying this particular cross." What must it have been for her? What was her attitude?

As I said, I got an insight as to possibly what that attitude might be a few years ago, when a woman came to see me. She had just gone through a lot of crosses herself, and she was now, she said, with a heart problem. Her husband had lost his executive job in a big corporation about a year and half ago, and then just two months ago, he had died of cancer. And I tried to comfort her as best I could, but she kind of stopped me and cut through it all with, I thought, a rather remarkable statement. She said, "I don't want to hear any of this, because you know what God told me? One day when I was just so angry, God said to me, 'Why should you be spared the crosses of life that everyone else must go through?' And I thought about that," she said, "and one day I said to God, 'You have forgiven me, now I forgive you.' "

And that was a remarkable statement. What does she mean that "she forgave God"? Well, she was angry at God for the crosses she had to carry. She was mad. She lived a good life, and this is the way she was treated. But basically, she was saying she forgave God because she didn't always perceive behind that supposed silence God's compassion, love, and ultimately, God's promise that through the crosses, her life would be shaped for the better.

And that brings us basically, I think, to the question that the gospel asks. How has the cross shaped your life? And I think this woman in the gospel is acting out an answer. That's what we have in Mark's story. We have a woman with a twelve-year cross. And I think in those twelve years, if she's a normal, average person, she wavered in fighting with this mystery—between love and hate, hope and despair, anger and frustration, peace and anxiety. I think she really struggled and was angry with God and wondered why she would have this particular cross in life. And I think the gospel incident that we have at hand indicates that at one point in her life, like this other woman, she decided to forgive God because she recognized that even though she had crosses, the cross had shaped her life in a peculiar way. By that I mean the cross made her, in some ways, possibly bitter, but also better.

You think of the experience of human life. It perhaps is the blind person who has developed a sensitivity to listen to the heartbeat of others. It is the crippled person who has great empathy for those who are deformed in body and mind. It is the

recovered alcoholic who is sensitized to the difficulties and the
power of addiction. It is the parent with a retarded child who
doesn't make fun of other retarded children or adults. It is the
person carrying the cross of sickness who can touch the brow
of the hospital patient with power. It is the one who has been
through a divorce and victimized through poor relationships
who knows how to heal broken hearts, or at least share courage.

In other words, you look over your life—everybody in this
building here—and you ask: "How has this cross shaped my
life?" In one sense crosses are horrible things. But ask yourself:
"If I didn't have this cross—difficulty at home, suffering a loss,
the death of a spouse, death of my children, someone who left
the faith, someone who's addicted to drugs—if I didn't have
them, what kind of a person would I be? Different from what I
am now?"

I don't know the answer to that, but the one thing I do know
about you is that you're here. Now why are you here with the
crosses you have? How has the cross shaped your life? Made
you who you are? And I think this is what happened to this
woman. When Jesus came along there was a turning point in
her life; and for the first time, she went up to God, in Jesus,
and instead of pounding her fist on God's chest, she forgave
God—and embraced Jesus' feet. She forgave God in the sense
that she should have realized that all along God was behind
everything—suffering with her, mortified with her, humiliated
with her, but loving her into something better through her
cross.

And although she could have, like people we know, turned
exceedingly bitter and angry at God, and shoved God out of
her life forever, still the cross brought her to her knees and she
recognized that through the cross somehow, by the love of
God, she became, in many ways, a better person. We express it
in our modern parlance that "there's no gain without pain."

There's no growth without the cross. You and I hate the
cross. Who wants to be sick and who wants to have a marriage
broken or who wants to have a wayward child? Nobody.

But—if it keeps you on your knees, crying out to God, even in anger, if it forces you to prayer, if it makes you scream, at least I suppose when your time comes, it's better to be found on your knees, forgiving God, than standing tall, pounding on God's chest.

So she touched the Lord and said, "I'm not going to fight it anymore." She touched the Lord and said, "I've been angry with you for lo, these twelve years." But when Jesus came along there was some kind of insight and she saw the flip side of her cross—the growth side, the positive side, the sensitizing side, the humanizing side, the loving side, the giving side, the heroic side—which she would never have achieved without her cross. And I think that's the point at which she just said, "I've got to touch him differently." So put yourself, perhaps, in that position. Look into the hurts, the sicknesses, the disappointments of your life.

And ultimately, therefore, the meaning of this gospel, I think, comes down to this. It's a gospel not of a miracle story (in fact, two miracles)—I think it is a gospel of invitation. All of us, with our crosses, have a chance to encounter God. And God is perfectly content if we rant and rave and are angry with him. All good relationships have that, and God is in relationship with us. God doesn't mind that. But the gospel is also an invitation to look at our cross, the thing that we're carrying that's bothering us right now; and it's an invitation to ask, "How has it shaped my life?"

How indeed?

Look over the past years, even those of you who are young. How have the failures made you a better person? How have the disappointments brought you to your knees? How have the hurts at least given you a certain humility—to know that ultimately everything's in God's hands anyway? How have the troubles and the addictions, the broken hearts, given you a better sensitivity with humankind? You're being invited—after enough of the shouting at God, God is asking for your forgiveness. Forgive God for what you thought God was like, and embrace God for what God is.

19

+

No More Wine

John 2:1–11

As always, in John's gospel there are many layers of meaning and symbol. And there are probably around a dozen or more ways to unpack all of the symbols that he has. But I think we might reflect not on all of the deep symbolism that John has there, but rather on a very prosaic sentence that is in the beginning of the gospel, one that most of us here today could resonate with.

They're midway through the wedding feast and the mother of Jesus comes to him and says, "They have no more wine." You think about that. That becomes a great symbol. And I've heard it and you've heard it repeated many times, many times.

The excitement, the joy, the festivity—suddenly they're over. The wine runs out. Or as we Americans like to express it in a more popular way, "the honeymoon is over." The school is a good school, but now you're getting bogged down in exams and term papers. The job is an exciting job, but there are now long stretches of boredom and the challenge is gone. The friendship is true, but little misunderstandings put stresses on it—it's not what it was fifteen years ago. The marriage is good—or was good—but somewhere along the line, the wine ran out.

Faith was sustaining when things were going well, but when my husband died, or my child got sick, things turned a little bit sour; and the wine, again, ran out. Hope was easy to talk to somebody else about who was in despair, but when they told me I had that terrible sickness, the wine ran out. Love is great as long as it endures and grows, but at the point it stopped growing and stopped enduring, the wine ran out.

And so this one resonance you and I can make. You look at your lives or the lives of people that you have known; at your losses, both necessary and unnecessary. You look into the mirror and you hear yourself saying, "I have no more wine."

The gospel comes along at this point in people's lives and says this: Jesus enters here and he not only enters, but he enters with the power to transform. Not in the Pollyanna sense—that everyone will be smiling and tripping over daisies—but in the sense that he has the power to draw wine from the bland water we have now been content to drink. He comes with the message that even though we have had disaster and hurt and betrayal, growth and fulfillment can rise from that. He comes with the message that says like all good wine, this wine needs time to ferment, to become vintage; and if we only have patience, he has the vintage waiting for us.

To this extent, we're asked by the gospel to believe that Jesus Christ will come and he'll transform your life and mine, and make things new again, and that he will be the master. So then we ask ourselves, "Do people really believe this? I mean, it would be nice if it happened, but do they believe it?"

And there's another thing in John's gospel that gives a very sensitive answer, I think. Even though Jesus performed the miracle and he turned the water into wine, nevertheless he had the help of the servants. He said, "Tell the servants to come and draw water and pour it into these jugs." If they did not do that, then there was no miracle, no transformation. And therefore, I think the message of the gospel is not only that Jesus can transform the loss, the boredom, the pain, the betrayal, that any of us feel; not only can he restore the hope that we once knew, and feel the love that has gone out of our lives; not only can Jesus do that, but he asks us necessarily, to help with the miracle.

I want to share with you two true stories—one is from India and the other is from Chicago, two places about as far apart as you can get.

The one involves a man whose name you might know if you read a certain book that was a bestseller a few years ago. His name is Stephen Kowaski. Stephen was born about 1933 in a little village in Poland. When he was about five years old, because there was no work there, his family moved to France in search of work. There his father became involved in some kind of labor unions. He was involved in some kind of altercation with the police. He was arrested, and he died in jail.

Stephen grew up and joined a seminary. He joined a little order that nobody knows about called the Fraternity of Saint Vincent. In any case, his superiors asked him to go to India to begin a small community among the poor. But he had to wait awhile there in France, waiting for his visa and things like that; and while he was there he worked among the poor North African immigrants.

He finally got to India, and once there he settled in Calcutta in a section that is no bigger than three football fields, into which seventy thousand people are crowded. It is with some irony known as the City of Joy, and that's the name of the book that was the bestseller a few years ago. A magnificent book—very touching book.

Well, Stephen moved into a one-room hovel in a slum. He had a slight bit more room than the average citizen. The total sum of his room was three square feet.

Most of the people worked from seven o'clock in the morning until ten o'clock at night. They got two rupees a day, not enough to feed them even a meager meal once a day. Some flocked there because the crops had failed, some because the landlords had driven them out, some because of poverty. Whatever it was, there were seventy thousand people crowded probably in the area of a church building with a couple of acres of property.

It was there in that slum that Stephen began his life among unbelievers. There were very few Christians. Most of them were Muslims and Buddhists, and they all shared together the squalor of Calcutta.

Every morning Stephen arose and waited in line for one of the ten water fountains from which people drew the water to wash. He cooked his simple meals and often shared them with those who had none.

In his small, three-square-foot hovel, he had that picture, you know, of the face of Jesus from the Shroud of Turin; and every single day Stephen spent, and still to this day spends, hours in prayer before that icon. And that prayer and that practice convinced his hostile neighbors that he, indeed, believed in a God who cared about the poor and the oppressed. And over the years, therefore, they came to trust him and even allowed him, which is very difficult in that hostile religious climate, to talk to them about religion.

But most of all what comes across through the book is this: that people came to understand that this man lived among them only because he loved them. There was no other earthly reason why someone who was a well-do-do, accepted, white man—who could live an easy and comfortable life—would chose freely to live in that hovel, in their dirty, filthy oppressed lives, squeezed in with seventy thousand of them. There was no other earthly motivation except that he loved them. And from there, they made the significant jump—that if Stephen Kowaski could live among them and love them that much, then so must God love them and live among them as well.

This is a classic example of where people whose wine had run out in every which way found the presence of Jesus to transform their lives. And so although they live in utter poverty and want, and sleep in the streets, the City of Joy has a new ring to it because Jesus Christ is there; because Stephen Kowaski is there.

I think that's what John is trying to tell us. For those of you whose wine has run out, Jesus can transform your life, but he needs the help of a few servants to do that.

Think of the ones you know who are lonely and bored, who are sick and despised, who are dying of terrible diseases, who are going through the pain of divorce, who have been rejected. Their wine has run out. It's the Stephen Kowaskis of this world who make wine flow again.

The other true story is interesting and more journalistic. It's from Chicago, and the interesting thing here is that the fastest-growing Christian church in the United States is in a suburb of Chicago, South Barrington. They get about twelve thousand people a week to worship, so they had to build a big hall—like a big amphitheater. Imagine twelve thousand people a week.

But what we're interested in is that of those twelve thousand, five to six thousand of them are former Catholics. It's the Willow Creek Community Church. And so seeing this (and I have to give them credit —it's like J.C. Penney asking Sears how come they're so successful), the archdiocese of Chicago went and asked the pastor there, a very fine fellow named Bill Hybles, "What's the secret of your success? How come you're drawing so many people, not to mention a good many Catholics?" He said, "Yes, 40 to 50 percent of my congregation are former Catholics." He said, "I work it this way. I use modern marketing techniques. As modern marketing does (some of you know this better than I), I went from door to door and researched. And I asked people, 'Why don't you attend church?'"

Now here are the half dozen answers he received. See if you resonate with any of these answers, or if you've got your seventh one. And the people, your neighbors and friends right now who are home reading the *Times* and not here—why don't they attend church?

In order of frequency the answers were:

1. They're always asking for money.
2. I don't like the music.
3. I can't relate to the message.
4. It doesn't meet my needs.
5. The services are predictable and boring.
6. They make me feel guilty.

These were the answers Bill Hybles got. So he said, like a good marketer, "Well, we've got to respond to these realities here." And so he had an approach, and I'd like to share his approaches very quickly, as to why he's so successful. He said to Cardinal Bernardin, the archbishop, "You oughta try it. You'll like it."

"First of all," he said, "because most people are highly insulated from any kind of Christianity in society, it is important that someone who is a believer builds a relationship with them" You hear what he's saying? This is true. He's on target. People are insulated from Christianity in our popular, official society, from school to public life. No reference to God, much less to Christianity's version of things, is permitted or allowed. The media, the press, the magazines in your book rack right now, are devoid totally of the spiritual and of Christianity.

Therefore, the only way to reach these people, since the mass media are paganized and secular, is that someone who is a believer establish a relationship with them. Now you see how that relates to the gospel—what I said about Stephen Kowaski. The hostile Muslims over there now have a relationship to the life of this man who prays hours a day in front of the image of Jesus Christ. They have built a relationship and they have come to know Jesus because of Stephen.

Bill Hybles is saying that people will be believers because of Mary and Mike and Joe and Alice, who are here. There is no other way. Do you build a relationship with others so that what you have you can share? So that you can fill again the cups of those whose wine has run out?

Secondly, he says that such believers must give actual verbal witness to these people. They're not afraid of that, but Catholics are afraid. The witnesses of Bill Hybles's church establish relationships, and sooner or later they say, "My faith means this to me. 'Nobody know the troubles I've seen,' as the old spiritual goes, but Jesus came into my life and made wine out of water." So do you do that? Are you afraid of intruding? These people aren't.

Third, those who have given verbal witness then should

invite the others to a Sunday service. Have you ever invited anybody to worship with you? Really, you think about that. And if not, they're going to go thirsty.

Fourth, then you invite them to a more in-depth Wednesday night service: A renewal group, some education, adult ed.

Fifth, he said, you get them into small groups—like our renewal groups, support groups, Bible study groups, and you establish friendships.

And sixth, he said, you get them involved in ministry; and finally you turn them over to recruit other people. A very simple marketing device used for the gospel.

And that is in line with the gospel: "...they have no wine." Jesus just doesn't stand there. He says, "O.K., servants, will you help?" And if they didn't help, he was powerless, in the sense that without their help he didn't have the water in front of him to transform. If you bring him the water he will make all things new again.

There are a lot of people, as you know, who are content with water. There are others, as you know, who stand before the world with broken hearts, and say, "I have no more wine." There are people who are despised and hurting—physically, mentally, emotionally, and God knows, spiritually. And John says, "But Jesus is the answer." Do you believe that? Jesus is not the answer in some simplistic way, but Jesus can transform.

Any one of us here can at least be a witness to Jesus. Do we spend, not maybe three or four hours, as Stephen does, before the image of Jesus Christ, but ten minutes or fifteen minutes in prayer? Do we remember in our prayer, by name, those whose cups are empty? Whose lives may be full of things but simply devoid of relationships?—which is a terrible way to live. What are we doing about witnessing? Can we at least invite someone to worship with us, and say at least, "Come and see"? Can't we at least invite them to come and listen to God's word, open up their hearts, and come with a receptive mind?

So the gospel is more than about a wedding. The gospel is about emptiness; and people are dying of emptiness in our country—more spiritual than physical. You alone have the key. Not that you have to be a fanatic and drive people wild, but you have to be convinced that Jesus Christ has power. You have to be convinced that Jesus can transform.

When people come to you and say they have no more wine, there's something you can do to fill that void. You can assist the Lord with the miracle of transformation. You can pray. You can invite. You can bear witness. There is so much that can be done.

So you and I are now going to go back to our ancient meal, and we're going to break the bread and share the cup with one another because we're a people of God. And as we do, think of all the people for whom that piece of bread would be so nourishing to their spirit, and for whom that wine, now become the blood of Christ, would be so saving to their hearts.

20

+

Freeing the Voice

Mark 7:31–38

This is a heavy-laden gospel. Maybe I can share some of this hidden insight by reference to a well-known Irish play called Translation. It's a story about what happens to a people when not only the rule, but the language of a foreign nation, are imposed upon them.

As a human symbol of all this, the play opens with a hedge-school teacher (you know the hedge-school teachers in old Ireland were the people who used to grab the children and hide them in the hedges and teach them their heritage because the British forbade them to teach their language and their culture) who is coaxing and encouraging a young woman to overcome her speech impediment; and at least to learn to say her own name. Her agonized struggle to form simple words that express her identity are finally successful, and she is transformed in her face, which shows a new dignity that at last she can publicly profess her identity and who she is.

But in the last act of the play, there is a bullying military officer of the occupying force who has gathered these people, this young girl included, to interrogate them because an officer has been killed and he suspects that some of them are harboring the killers. She is so frightened and intimidated by his bullying ways that once more she loses the power of speech. And it becomes clear, as you watch the play, that the girl is not only the girl, but she represents all the people who have been rendered dumb by the violation of their culture. Not only that, but those who chose to accept for safety's sake the alien culture become deaf to their own people's needs.

And so when you watch this Irish play, you begin slowly to understand that it becomes a parable. It's a parable of what happens to a group of people who are oppressed and used by another group that is more powerful. And this, of course, is where Mark's gospel comes in because at the time of Jesus, as you know, his people were occupied by an alien force, the Roman army. The nation was ruled by a power that not only imposed a foreign rule, but also worse than that, imposed a language and a symbol and a label; and there were those who collaborated with the Romans; and the moment they adopted their language and their culture and their labels, they became insensitive to their own oppressed people. The oppressed people, in turn, no longer clearly knew who they were because they were not allowed, like this girl, to form the words of their identity. In order to survive they had to speak the language of the oppressor and to accept the meaning that the oppressors gave them, as simple, ignorant outcasts. They could no longer speak their own name as a people of God.

So it is with any subjugated people. As with any subjugated people, they cannot celebrate their festivals; that's the first thing an occupying force does. You cannot celebrate a festival (like Catholics were not allowed to celebrate Christmas in their way in the early colonial days of America). They cannot sing their songs. They cannot recite their poetry. They cannot tell of their heroes and heroines. They cannot relate their stories. And the hope is that in due time they will forget who they are, and they will begin to accept and act out the labels that their oppressors have put on them. We have that in all kinds of history: "I am nothing. I am no good. I am nobody." You see that in the great Afro-American spirituals—"I am just an orphan, a motherless child."

It's something like one of the stories by Alice Walker, who

wrote *The Color Purple*. She has an interesting short story called
"Meridian." A little black girl down in the South is playing in
the yard, and she finds this piece of metal. She recognizes that
this piece of metal is a bar of gold, and she digs up this incredible, heavy bar of gold. She rushes home to her mother, who is
sitting on the back porch, shelling peas. She says, "I found some
gold." And she places the large, heavy gold bar in her mother's
lap. Her mother says, "Move that thing out of the way. Don't
you see I'm trying to get supper ready?" "But it's gold," she in-
sists. "Feel how heavy it is. Look how yellow it is. It's gold. It
could make us rich." But her mother was not impressed and her
father was not impressed; and her brothers and sisters were not
impressed; and the neighbors were not impressed. So she is rejected, and no one is interested in sharing her joy. So she takes
her bar of gold, and she puts it in a shoebox and she buries it
under the magnolia tree in the backyard; and once a week she
digs it up and holds the bar of gold in her lap. Then, less and
less. It's once a month, until finally she forgets to dig it up at all.
And she acted like everyone else, not as someone possessing a
bar of gold.

When I say these things, you probably think that I have in
mind only political oppression. But I do not. I think the gospel
is a remarkably profound statement about religious and cultural oppression. For example: When I was flipping the dial on
the television looking for a newscast, I picked up a very quick
segment of one of those comedies that's set in a law court. In
this very brief episode, one woman was accusing another
woman of being a virgin; and she was enormously embarrassed and upset and protested vigorously that she, of course,
was not. And I thought to myself, although this is just a comedy, she's still a symbol of a person who's oppressed. You see,
she had a label that the culture had imposed on her. You cannot speak of virginity without a laugh or a smile or a snicker.
Fidelity has been replaced by Sylvester Stallone's and Liz Tay-
lor's lifestyles. In that kind of culture you cannot speak of fidelity and be taken seriously.

In spite of the fact that every poll from Gallup to Harris

shows that Americans are an extremely religious people; in spite of the fact that there's a high church-goingness by this crowd in America; despite the fact that 95 percent of the people believe in God and about 85 percent of them pray daily—the mass media will never discover any one of them at prayer. And people in the movies or on television don't sign themselves with the sign of the cross unless they are ignorant Hispanics or superstitious Irish. It is low comedy to do that.

Religious discourse is forbidden in any public or government-funded place, and in public schools in the United States no symbol, sign, or mention of God may be named. And God and religion, therefore, are relegated to the sensational and bizarre, by courtesy of Winfrey, Donahue, and other talk show hosts.

Sixty-five percent of our Catholic youth have no religious education after confirmation. They cannot recite the Ten Commandments or the spiritual or corporal works of mercy. They have forgotten their language. They are struck dumb. And those who accept the alien culture—the secular culture—then become indifferent to their own people: "I have it made. Why should I care about others?" (They say this in spite of the fact that lately our environment has begun protesting in a loud voice that if we don't care about others we hurt them and ourselves as well.)

And so the people both young and old (and you see the power of this gospel) begin to lose their voice. They forget their faith stories. They no longer sing sacred songs; they sing secular songs. They become deaf to their heritage and they are forced to live by the labels that the culture places on them. And what are the labels of our commercial-consumer culture? That you are fat and ugly. You have the wrong clothes. You live in the wrong neighborhood. You smell bad. You drink the wrong wine cooler and are not driving this year's "in" car. You are nothing unless you speak the language of the culture.

And so people raise the volume of their music to drown out the absence of God. They give fidelity to the tube; they spend life collecting; they fill their lives with drugs and take their lives in alarming numbers.

But Mark's gospel comes along and says that Jesus Christ is like that hedge-teacher, coaxing and encouraging all of us to say who we really are. To speak once more the ancient language, that "I am made in the image and likeness of God; that I count; and that someone, someone truly loves me unconditionally—no strings attached. Doesn't look at my house or my clothes; just looks me in the heart and loves me."

That we live by more than bread alone. That there is a love to share. That there are hungry to feed. That it is by dying to self that we truly live. That there is a meaning to life—and it is to love God and one's neighbor as one's self. That there is worship in a faith community such as our own. That there is a Christ in the breaking of the bread, and that love overcomes all things, even death. That there's a whole language and a whole story and whole song beyond the Christmas commercials we'll be hearing again this year.

And I think in a particular way, and a significant way, accidentally, that this is a most powerful gospel for parents and for faith-filled adults. Because every faith-filled adult and every parent here must see himself and herself as a hedge-school teacher. And you must whisper the old memories into the ears of the young. You must unlock their voices so they can reclaim their identity as children of God. You must liberate them and give them their voice, and their worth, and their meaning.

So Mark was saying something more than a little miracle story. He's saying this man who had his tongue tied and was deaf is a symbol of Israel. That the alien culture had impressed its labels and values and the Israelites were suffocating; and they forgot their songs. And those who collaborated with the oppressors made their compatriots feel inferior, and Jesus came and said, "Be opened."

And that's what you and I are about; and that's why you're here, in this holiday time, as Christmas approaches. You are a powerful sign. You are trying to be reborn and renewed in this liturgy so that you can lay your hands on those near and dear to you. And you can whisper Jesus' heartfelt words, "Be opened." Open to God, open to life, open to love.

21

✛

All Saints

Revelation 7:1–8

For almost two thousand years people have written about what we call "the beatitudes."

There really hasn't been a consensus on precisely how they are to mean something to us. Are they impossible principles that we strive for—ideals of some sort? Are they practical things to try to live with? Are they just little aphorisms that have been collected and strung together? People have never quite been sure.

But one thing that does seem certain is that when you have sayings attributed to a person, the sayings usually reveal the nature of that person. If, for example, Ben Franklin talked about "a stitch in time saves nine" and "a penny saved is a penny earned," we know, in fact, that he was indeed a very frugal person. His clever little sayings reveal something of himself.

And so these sayings of Jesus, however we interpret them, reveal a great deal about him. As you go down the list of the beatitudes, you have, in fact, people who have fallen through the cracks of human life; and, in effect, Jesus is saying, "I'm concerned about these people, too. They have my compassion, they have my thoughts, and they have my concern, and my blessing."

And so he speaks to his disciples, and he's talking about the
poor, the sorrowing, the lonely, the hungry, the thirsty, the single-hearted, the peacemakers, and the persecuted. All those
people who don't quite make it in life. All these people who
somehow are basically not "with it," out of the mainstream.
And yet he says, "This is my concern," and the implication is
that "this is what you should be about as well." So these beatitudes reveal something of the heart and mind of Jesus.

But the scope of God's concern is even wider than that. In
that first reading, you witness the very grand and panoramic
sweep of John's vision. He speaks of the countless holy ones—
he says 144,000. Well, of course, the biblical number of fulfillment and perfection is twelve and this says, "Boy, this is
twelve times twelve—perfection times perfection. You can't
count the number of people that are among the holy ones."

And this in turn reveals something about God as well, because the Feast of all Saints is basically a feast not only of the
compassion of Jesus, who is concerned about the marginal, it is
about the love of God that is so universal and beyond our
wildest dreams that, as the reading says, It has found the way
to redeem "people from every race, language and walk of life,
perfection times perfection, countless upon countless." And so
it would seem that among those countless, countless people
are those who hunger and thirst, the persecuted, the lonely,
the meek, the single-hearted.

It seems, therefore, that as we reflect upon this feast and
tend to think only of the great saints and the saints that we
have known in our lives, we should not forget to go behind it
always. And behind it is this incredible love of God which is so
vast it can collect 144,000 people, and is so deep that it will slip
between the cracks and get even the marginal. So this is a reflection about All Saints. It's not just all these wonderful people that we trip off in our litanies. It is the feast, as every feast
is, of God. It's a feast of God's love. It is horizontal, if you will,
and it is vertical. And the feast of All Saints and the Feast of
All Souls, and putting the Beatitudes on this Feast of All
Saints, are meant to tell us that truth.

Beyond our wildest imaginings God's love will find what we could never find, redeem what we would think is irredeemable, and collect what we would throw away—144,000 from every tribe, countless upon countless upon countless—to the exponent that we could not begin to measure with the most sophisticated computer.

This is the feast of God's love and, therefore, a feast of hope. If God's love is that extensive, and if God's love is that vertical, if God's love will go to the marginal and the in-between people, then it turns this feast of great admiration for God, and worship, also into a feast of hope. So maybe today as we go about our daily business, we just might contemplate how marvelous God's love is. How wildly wide, how profoundly deep, how incredibly comprehensive, how wonderful must this God of ours be.

22

✝

The Good Woman

Luke 18:20–22

I'm not especially a tennis buff but I saw a headline recently which made me read on further. The headline simply said, "From Court to Convent." It was a story of a Canadian athlete, a young woman named Vera Komar. Those of you who do know tennis know the name. She never reached the great superstar status of some of those incredible women tennis players in the seventies, but she was a junior tennis player and then she turned professional.

She took part in all the tournaments across the world, often entering the quarter-finals and the semifinals, but she herself never became one of the superstars. She had kind of a bumpy time and as you know, being on the circuit, going all over the world, playing and living out of hotel rooms and suitcases really is not as glamorous as portrayed. It's king of a rough life, always enroute and never settling down.

Well, in Vera's case, after doing the world circuit and being a rather good and respectable player, in spite of the fame and the money, she began to feel a disquietude. And two things, the story reveals, began to happen to her that made a great change in her life. One, she was in St. Peter's Square in Rome in one of the great general audiences; and as she described it, she suddenly felt an enormous sense of the presence of God. One of those rather common mystical experiences that happen to people often enough. She just had that sudden realization and that moment of harmony and peace and felt that presence.

Then a little later on, when she was kind of off the circuit and somewhat broke, discouraged and not feeling well, one of the priests that she talked to thought that she needed a rest and suggested that she spend a few days with the Trinitarian nuns in one of the Roman convents. She did so. And spending the few days kind of getting a mental and emotional rest, she observed the great work that the sisters did with the homeless of Rome. The combination of that experience of the presence of God plus the experience of these dedicated women who did not have any fame or fortune, but simply went out to the streets, literally, of Rome, and took care of the homeless women, moved her deeply.

And she made a change in her life, and she quit the tennis circuit, and she is now one of these Trinitarian nuns—very happy, unknown; quietly giving herself to others. So that was what's behind the headline "From Court to Convent."

But I think what particularly struck me, that ties into this Advent season, was that this is the story of a young woman who has not made a radical change in the sense that she was a wicked, wicked person. We always like those kinds of stories. Like St. Augustine, who turned from horrible sin to sanctity. But she is rather like you and me, and I think that this is what makes her appealing. She is not a scarlet woman. She's not a reprobate. She's not an evil person. She's not wickedness personified; but rather, she's a good person. But a good person who made a change in her life.

And I think that means more to us because that's our category. There are very few of us who are wicked and scarlet and wild. We're good people. But because of being good people, we often kind of turn aside the voice that calls us further. I came across the prayer of a man named Michel Quoist, who writes some very fine things, and his prayer goes like this:

Lord, here I am, not feeling sinful.
I don't do dreadful things like stabbing
people, stealing or mugging. I try to
help people and love them. I suppose I
don't help the right people in the right
way. Probably I trust myself more than
you. So help me to see what you would
like changed in me. There must be
something. Help me to feel sinful, if this
is what you want.

You see the point of his prayer. The point of his prayer is that he's a good man. He keeps the commandments. He loves his neighbor. He goes to church on Sunday. He's good. But he also suspects that that goodness is kind of a shield from deeper commitment to prayer and to love and to mission. And he speaks, therefore, on behalf of good people like this Vera Komar. What would God want changed in my life, as a good person during this Advent? That's the question that comes out of the scripture.

What does a prophet like John the Baptist say to me? What does repentance mean to me? Not repentance from a horrible life to a good life, but rather the repentance from a good life to something deeper. You see, what John and the scripture are saying to us is that we carry within us a subtle defense against deeper holiness. We could all probably say, "Well, I can make my confession here in front of everybody, and I guess outside of the usual human failings, I'm a good person. I really don't go around mugging people and stabbing them." But then, you see, we treat God in the negative. "I don't do the horrible things, therefore I'm relieved from doing the better things."

And the scripture confronts us and won't let us get away with that. And people like Vera Komar, who are good people, say, "Are you listening to something better, more profound?" Her story is of a good woman who changed, not an evil woman who converted. And that's our message. As good people, what would God really like changed in our lives? Where could we be called to a deeper level? A profound holiness and difference. And we can make a difference.

I was reading the other day somewhere—and I forget what part of the Harvard University Institute this is—but these futurists look ahead, of course—that's their business. And they say—this is very interesting to me and I want to develop it sometime—that there are four international, global realities (if I can remember the four) that have, and will have, an impact on the future of this globe. Let's see if I can remember what they were. One was the United Nations as a global institution. The other was the multinational corporations. They are global—all over the world. The third one escapes me now, but the fourth one, interestingly, was the Roman Catholic church, as one of the four global, influential bodies in the world that transcends all boundaries.

And so it's a moment when we can have great influence, when we can make a difference—the good people in the world. These people up at Harvard see the Catholic church as one of the four very persuasive and very meaningful ways that we can make a difference in this world—we can help determine whether we survive or not. And I would maintain that that difference is going to be made, not by mass conversions of the wicked, but rather the deeper Christianity of the good.

So this is a subtle message. I hope I'm getting it across. It's a subtle message because, as I say, it's about the way that we keep God from getting into our lives too deeply. Good people like ourselves have a way of making excuses for not being better because we always talk in the negative. "Well, I don't go around stealing cars," and "I'm not selling cocaine to three year olds," and that sort of thing. So therefore I'm good.

The word of God says, "Yes, but there's something lacking yet. There's something that can be changed." There's a deeper commitment to justice and peace. There is a deeper prayer life. There is a deeper centering of what God wants in your life and how God speaks to you. There is a more profound charity. There is even sacrifice to be made as we readjust certain things in our lives so that we can be more prophetic and holy and have an impact on this world.

So when you picture, as in today's Scripture, this great prophet, John the Baptist, and as you hear in the Scripture that John stands in the desert with his might, his thunderous power, calling all these wicked people to repent, don't be put off by that. It's not just the wicked. My suspicion is that a bigger impact is the conversion of the good, the deepness of the good, the profound prayer life of the good. My conviction is that the hope of this world is not if Gorbachev becomes a Catholic and is baptized by the pope. My conviction is that the salvation of the world is sitting here before me—the good people who listen to God's voice and become better.

23

Companions

1 Kings 19:1–9

The other day I heard the story of a football coach from an unnamed university in the Midwest; he was experiencing one of those terrible horrors of consistently losing. So, by mid-October the alumni were up in arms and out for blood, and to cap it all off, in early November his team lost to their traditional great archrivals in a resounding defeat. And so the next day the coach received a telegram which read, "The last train out of town leaves Sunday at noon; be under it."

You can transfer that to today's first reading, and it has, I think, a good message for us.

The first reading tells us about the great prophet, Elijah. And however great a prophet he is, he is simply at the end of his tether. He has been punished; he's wandering out into the desert; things are going badly; and that most wicked queen, Queen Jezebel, with all the wrath of Bette Davis, is after him. You can imagine why, in the first reading, he goes out there, sits under the broom tree, and prays to God that God would take his life. He is a beaten, and he is a defeated, man.

I think what's significant is the response. And after all, when you think about it, the ancient peoples had all kinds of stories: poems and legends and histories, and all that kind of thing, and you begin to wonder why they saved this story. What did they see in it that was more than the surface-story value? I think one clue is this: the way they tell it, when Elijah prayed to God that he was a defeated man, was at this end, asked God to take his life away, the response God made was to leave him a piece of bread. Not only once, but when he ate the hearth bread he fell asleep, and again, the next day, God's angel woke him up and the second time there was this little hearth bread there. And the meaning of that became clear to Elijah, as it was to the ancient peoples.

Most of you know that the Latin word for bread is *panis*. The Latin for "with" is *cum*. When you combine *cum* and *panis*, we get our English word "companion" from that. A *cumpanis*, or companion, is one who breaks bread with you; or as we would say, symbolically, is with you. And this is what the scripture lesson was in this passage. The ancient people of Israel saved it because it was about their understanding of God. It wasn't about some other people's understanding of God, the magic god who waves a wand and gives you an instant solution. Later on, God didn't even do that for Jesus. But the story of Jesus and the story of Elijah and the story of the tradition, is that God gives strength and companionship, not necessarily solutions.

The way this life works is that the most upbeat of us know that we will have troubles in life; and even though none of us wants difficulties and hardships, sickness, or family troubles, the fact is that we also instinctively know the old saying that "without pain there's no gain," that there's something written into human nature that says that we are made strong through adversity; our mettle is tried. And those of you who are parents, you don't even ultimately, really, try to take every stumbling block away from your children, but what you do want to do is to give them the message, "Son (Daughter), no matter what happens, remember Mommy and Daddy love you", or, in other words, "We are with you."

And when people know that people are with them, then they can do a great deal. They don't mind, ultimately, the pain and the suffering and the thing that all of us fear most, death. It's not the death as much as maybe dying alone. As one old gentleman in the nursing home said, "I don't want to die alone like a sparrow in a winter hedge."

So, God comes along in this story and says, "I leave you bread, I leave this *cumpanis* to tell you, Elijah, that I'm not going to do way instantly with Jezebel or all the other problems that you're carrying in your heart, but I will be with you. I will be your companion, both to give you strength, and to make, ultimately, all things new again. I am not here to take away the problem; I'm here to carry it with you."

It's like that old legend, you know, the grandfather clock that had been in the family for generations, century after century, so to speak, ticking off the seconds and the minutes and the hours. And of course, the means of operation with a grandfather clock was a heavy weight that was suspended by a double chain. Well, one of the new generation, believing that the old clock could not bear such a load any longer, released the weight, and of course, immediately, the ticking stopped. Well, you might remember that the legend goes that the grandfather clock asked, "Why did you do that?" And the owner replied, "I wanted to lighten your burden." But the clock replied, "Please, put the weight back. That's what keeps me going."

And God understands that. None of us likes the cross or the weight, but this is what keeps us going. And God's promise is not to be a distant God who runs in at the last minute and gives all solutions; ours is not a God of solutions; ours rather is a God of presence. The significance, therefore, of the bread left for Elijah is the promise of a lover who says, "I'm sorry for your pain, but I'll hold your hand." And for most of us, that's pretty good.

And this is why the gospel picks it up and we in this tradition celebrate the eucharist. The *panis angelicus,* the bread of heaven, as Aquinas said. The bread which simply means that I'll be with you. Of all the ways that Jesus could have found to sustain his presence, it is both significant and in the line of Elijah, that he says that, "I will be with you and you will know me in the breaking of the bread." And that's how we know each other, too, isn't it?

We invite each other over to our homes, and we say, "Come and eat with us; come to dinner," the highest form of intimacy; and when we break bread, we share a lot. We have no power to remove our companions problems, we just have the power, that incredible power, to be with them.

I think of Henry Francis Light (some of you might know the name), who was a minister, and had gone to a little fishing village; and because he was really a good man and got to know the people and got a Bible on every boat, and that sort of thing, his parish increased and people were all over the place. But early on, as a young man in his early fifties, he got very sick and the doctor told him he'd have to leave the place for a more benign climate. So he sat in his little garden overlooking the sea, thinking of the most recent few years, which hadn't been that good because of his sickness; he hadn't been able to be present and as a result some of the people had left the parish and had gone to other churches, and even those who remained were fighting among themselves. And yet, even in spite of that, he thought of all the good things and measured them out, and he wrote a song, a hymn, and it's probably one of the most consistent hymns in Protestant and Catholic missalettes that we have. He wrote the hymn "Abide with Me."

And again, the popularity of that hymn, "Abide with Me," resulted precisely because its message is so important to human beings. Otherwise people are unfulfilled. As I said before, it's not always answers that we need, or sometimes I suspect, it's not always answers that we want. I think all of us, knowing the restrictions of human existence, simply want a "cumpanion" to be with us. This is the essence of a good marriage, isn't it?

And the old people who made up the old vows knew that; and they did not have stars in their eyes. They said, "Hey, just because we're married doesn't mean that there's not child abuse or broken relationships and cancer and war; it's just that we'll walk together through these things, and if we can't conquer them, we'll overcome them by our mutual love." And so they were the ones, not the church or state or government, they're the ones who invented the words, "I take you for better or for worse"—will you walk with me then, in the valley of death? "For richer or poorer"—when I lose everything? "In sickness and in health"—will you hold my hand in my sickbed? That's what the vows are about. That's what companionship is about. That's what God is about. Otherwise you have people who walk through life hurting, not because they're oppressed by the unfairnesses and the poverties of life, but because they have no one who is companion.

I remember, years ago, reading a little biography of Moss Hart. You might remember his name—he was a well-known screen writer and a playwright, especially. He tells the story of when he was very small, about nine or ten years old, and very poor in New York. He and his dad were going out for some Christmas presents, and up on 149th Street they had a lot of those pushcarts; had all kinds of gifts and presents on them. Well, he was at an age when he had outgrown the toys, but his heart was set on either a printing set or a chemistry set. And so he describes how he and his father walked up and down, and every time the father looked at the price tag, they just moved on. And he writes these words: "My father had gotten together about seventy-five cents to buy me a Christmas present and he didn't dare say so in case there was nothing to be had for so small a sum. As I looked up at him, I saw a look of despair and disappointment in his eyes that brought me closer to him than I had ever been in my life. I wanted to throw my arms around him and say, 'It doesn't matter. I understand. *This* is better than a chemistry set or a printing press. I love you.' But instead, we stood shivering beside each other for a moment, then turned away from the last two pushcarts and started sadly back home. I didn't even take his hand on the way home, nor did he take mine. We were not on that basis. Nor did I ever tell him how close to him I felt that night; that for a little while the concrete wall between father and son had crumbled away, and I knew that we were two lonely people struggling to reach

each other." And that is probably life's greatest sadness, isn't it?

So, we go back to the Scripture. As always, it says something to us. It was saved for a reason, and the wisdom of the reason is, I think, that profound and magnificent answer of God to a beaten prophet. No silly, simple solution like soap operas give, but the promise, "I will be with you. I will be your companion. Here's the bread as a sign."

And when Jesus was about to leave us to go back to that same Abba, Father, he left us the eucharist with the same message. And of course, behind the message, then comes the invitation. The invitation that if we are to be disciples of the Lord, we must be companions to one another—as simply as that.

Translated, that means that this week there's somebody you can call; there's someone who's sick that you can drop a card to; there's someone who's lonely that you can say "hello" to; there is someone who is angry and hurting that you can touch; there is someone who is bitter and hurt that you can speak to; there is a family member who is turned in on himself or herself that you can be present to.

In other words, if we are to know how to live, we are being taught not to try to give solutions always; but simply to be present, to be Christ-like, to be nourishment, to be bread, to be companion.

24

Making Wishes Come True

Luke 4:14–19

It is our custom to do baptisms right during Mass, and as a part of that we ask the parents to share with the congregation what they would wish for their child.

Just think, for example, pretend you are new parents, and you have a three- or four-week-old baby, and you're standing here in front of everybody. What's the one thing that you wish for that child, if you could bring it about? Good health? Peace? Prosperity? Success? (However you define it.) What would it be?

I was thinking of that in reference to this gospel the other night, during a very beautiful, lovely confirmation. I was sitting up here looking out at ninety-five just marvelous young men and women, surrounded by those who are important to them, their parents, sponsors, relatives, and well-wishers, and I thought to myself, "If I were the collective parent of these fifteen-year-olds, what would I wish for them if I were forced to say one word?" And I thought of this gospel where it spoke in terms of power, in terms of servanthood, and the one word I came up with is: I would wish them "integrity."

Integrity meaning wholeness. You know, that you're a whole person. You say what you mean, you mean what you

say, and you run your life according to values. We say that "he
or she has integrity; you can't buy them off." And I thought of
the word "integrity" because not only is that a part of the gospel, but it's also a part of selfishness because it's a part of survival. These young people sitting in front of me, in twenty or
thirty years from now, will be running the world. They literally will be. And integrity is going to be, probably, the last boun-
dary as to whether we survive or not, literally.

I thought, therefore, we have to give them better role models, and how much the integrity is needed. Just looking over
the papers for one week, I see they've indicted Hertz Company, a big outfit like that, stealing millions from their customers
through deceitful practices. A senior Congressman from New
York, Mario Biaggi, is in jail for breaking the trust and for lack
of integrity, fundamentally. The whole HUD scandal, the overcharging at the Pentagon.* All these people lack integrity. And
perhaps the frightfulness came along when I was looking at
the paper, and whatever you saw on television, about the admission that a nuclear power plant in Ohio has been leaking
deadly poisons to the citizens of the world, and no one had
enough integrity to do anything about it, although a number of
people knew.

The opening paragraph in the paper says, "Government of-
ficials overseeing a nuclear weapons plant in Ohio knew for
decades that they were releasing thousands of tons of radioac-
tive uranium waste into the environment, exposing thousands
of workers and residents to danger." Representative Lukens,
who is heading the investigations, is quoted as saying this:
"The allegations against the Department of Energy in the court
action constitute a statement that the Department of Energy
was waging a kind of chemical warfare against the community. It admits that it knew for over twenty years that its waste
pits were leaking. It now admits that it knew that the plant's
pollution control system was obsolete and deteriorated for

---

*A massive scandal inside the United States government's Department of Housing
and Urban Development (HUD) came to light in the summer of 1989. Around the
same time it was revealed that a number of major defense contractors had been
overcharging the Pentagon.

years. And now it admits that it knew that heavy rains swept uranium-contaminated water into nearby streams and into the ground water that people drink. And most important of all, it now admits that for most of the last thirty-five years, it sat on its hands and did nothing to fix these serious and life-threatening problems."

Of course, you say, "That's the government," but the government is a fiction. The government is a collective name for human beings who run it. And someday, some of those ninety-five young men and women who were confirmed the other night will be in government, and will be on the board of some nuclear power plant in Ohio; and whether they have integrity or not, means whether the world, literally, survives or not.

And so that's why I pray for them, that they would have integrity, and better models than perhaps our generation has given them (or at least the ones that the media have glorified). And I thought if that's so, and if the media have glorified such amoral models for them, perhaps we as a faith community, and particularly parents, can offer them a different model.

So it seems to me that those of us who are gathered here each weekend, the thousands of us who come for church and worship—whether we are parents, or single, like myself, or divorced or separated, or whatever reason we're here—I think that we owe it to our young people's integrity to share with them three things. (I think that we don't do this enough, or maybe hardly at all—you have to ask yourself.)

First of all, do your young people know what you do? What *do* you do? Do your children know that? What do you do for a living? Are you a housewife; a househusband; a government official; work in a corporation; operate a gas station? What do you do?

Secondly, you should discuss with them how you do it. With competence? Under pressure? With difficulty? What's the talent you bring to it; what's the knowledge; what's the expertise?

And finally, and most critical of all: How does faith enter into your decisions? In my most ideal scenario, I can picture after a dinner, after a meal at night, the parents sitting around with the children, and the mother or father saying, "Look, I've got this problem at work. It's an ethical decision. If I don't do this I will not get promoted, or if I don't do this, I'm going to get fired. That means that you, Mary and Johnny, you may not be able to go to college; or I can't afford it. Let's discuss this. Let's talk about the fight, and the problems of values here." And I would think that when families talk together about values, or what they've just seen on television that is clearly amoral, then parents are giving their children integrity so that when they are your age, they will remember this lesson.

So there are three things we should share with the younger generation: What do we do? How do we do it? And how does faith enter into what we decide?

This may sound remote, but I tell you, twenty or thirty years will go by quickly, and it's only those with moral integrity who literally will save this planet. It will be people who make decisions about nuclear waste; people who will make decisions about selling cocaine to children or adolescents; people who will make decisions about abortion. It's people who make decisions that effect the lives of millions of workers. It is people who will make decisions to overcharge. Will your children be among them?

So as I sat there and I looked at these ninety-five young men and women, all looking so beautiful and wonderful, and tried to project in my mind twenty and thirty years from now when they have *power*, I asked myself, "Will the power be the power of the Spirit? And will those who surround them now—mom and dad, brothers and sisters, people like myself—will we have taught them well? And have shared with them these three questions of our lives?" The future literally depends on it.

I guess, on the bottom line, you're teaching them the gospel. "The one who would rule," Jesus says, "must be the servant of all." In our power-hungry society that measures success only, and exclusively, in terms of money, the gospel challenges that, and says there's another way to act and to live and to serve.

And so we have to help our children, our young people, find God. Even if they lapse, and even if they enter into a period when they turn their backs on God, I tell you, if you build that in early, those who lose God rediscover God in another way.

I remember an old movie, and it really is old, because you have to be a certain age to have remembered George Arliss, the great character. He was in a very interesting picture that I hope they replay on television sometime, called The Man Who Played God. It was the story of a very talented and very wealthy musician. He had the worst possible thing that could happen to a musician—he began to lose his hearing. He was going deaf. And so he became very bitter and very cynical. And not only did he turn his back on his friends, but he turned his back on God as well. Being rich, he moved into a penthouse, and there he took lessons in learning to read lips to compensate for his loss of hearing. In the movie, from his penthouse window, he overlooked a park. He would look through a pair of high-powered binoculars, and he would learn to read the lips of people. Well, one day he concentrated on the lips of a young man whose lips were moving in prayer; and so he determined what the young man was praying for, and being wealthy, he dispatched his butler to give the young man what he had been praying for. On another occasion he read the lips of a young woman who was telling her friend about something that she so desperately needed, and once again he dispatched his butler to fulfill that need. And each time he performed one of these services, the cynical musician would raise his face to heaven and he would laugh in God's face. He found it so humorous and so laughable that he was playing God; and he didn't even believe in God. But, of course, as you have already guessed, what happened is that in time, doing all these things, meeting people's needs, the man who played God, found God. And maybe that's what you have to build in early. That even in those periods when the people you love turn their backs on God, if you have trained them to have integrity and to be the servant of all; even when they don't believe in what they're doing but they serve their fellow human beings, they will rediscover God in a new way—I promise you that.

You may have your own prayer and gift that you would offer, but I thought integrity was probably the thing that any fourteen- or fifteen-year-old needs. Twenty-five years from now they will need it badly—so that they may survive.

So talk to them; model to them. Show them what you do and how you do it and how faith enters in. And help them once more to know, not only God, but someday to rediscover so powerfully that they, your children, our parishioners, will make a difference.

25

Taking Up Your Cross

Matthew 16:21–28

Some of you know the name, of course, of Tom Wolfe, the best-selling author. His book, *The Bonfire of the the Vanities*, was on the best-selling list, and headed it for fifty-six straight weeks.

In any case, it was Tom Wolfe who invented the phrase the "me generation" for the seventies. At the end of the eighties he was interviewed and was asked, "Well, if you call the seventies the 'me' generation, what about the eighties, and now the nineties, which are now just around the corner?"

He said, "If I were to characterize the eighties, my opinion is that it would be called the 'money fever' generation." And I guess that's easy to see with all of the shenanigans we've heard about and people being indicted on these multimillion dollar frauds; living high, things of that nature. Even the latest things with HUD*.

"Significantly," he said, "there was, about a few years ago, one of those mistakes that happen occasionally. They printed a certain amount of coins, which are now collectors items, and instead of 'In God We Trust' printed on the coin, it was 'In Gold We Trust.' "

---

*In the summer of 1989 a huge scandal involving bribes, cronyism, and misman-agement was uncovered inside the United States government's Department of Housing and Urban Development (HUD).

And he pointed also to an article in *TV Guide,* and I would like to quote to you from that article about the generation to come, and our children. It says:

> They live in a world in which only slightly more than a decade ago, the average supermarket carried nine thousand items and now carries twenty-four thousand. It's a world in which Revlon now makes one hundred fifty-eight shades of lipstick, in which there are thirty-six sizes and flavors of Crest toothpaste, and in which in about half of all American homes, there are more than twenty television channels to choose from.
>
> It's also a world in which it's harder for young people to define their sense of right and wrong because there are so many sources. Especially hard because so many of them don't hold firm. Schools don't impose values, parents are busy and confused themselves, and organized religion plays a smaller part in people's lives. There's been an erosion among the traditional suppliers of values. There's a vacuum, and so for many young people, television and their peers play a greater role.

So they asked Tom, "Well, in the light of the 'me generation' of the seventies, and the kind of 'greed generation' of the eighties, what do you see now for the nineties that are upon us?" He was reflective and said, I think insightfully, this: "I think the nineties are going to be characterized simply as the 'decade of relearning,' because people are now reacting to the excesses and they realize that there are certain values and certain fundamentals, and also, a thirst for God." So he foresees the nineties as a time of relearning some of the basic values that have sustained humankind for all these decades.

That has something to do with the gospel, in fact a great deal, because there's a phrase in there that is always a little bit puzzling. Jesus says to his disciples, "Look, unless you take up your cross daily and follow me, you're not worthy of the kingdom of heaven." And often in Christianity that phrase has been misinterpreted, and I think badly, because what comes across is that "look, everybody, we want you to be a Christian, and we promise you humiliation, pain, and suffering; so come and join us." Who would want to join an outfit like that? Especially in our pleasure conscious society which promises fulfillment from every car that you buy.

But that's to misinterpret Our Lord's words to "take up your cross daily." A cross, remember, is made up of two crosspieces—and so, therefore, it becomes the symbol of decision. You can go one way or the other; you're at the cross roads. The word "crisis" comes from that. And people who have a crucifixion are people who maybe make hard decisions and have to live tough hanging on them.

And this is what he means. "Unless you take up your cross daily, unless you make daily choices that make a difference, you're not worthy of me." That's the cross, and sometimes that's a far harder cross, in one way, than the physical suffering.

The point is, that if there is to be a time of relearning, there obviously needs to be a time of reteaching. And who are the better teachers in the world than right here before me? Let me give you some practical examples.

I was talking to a group who have formed what they call a "base community." Base communities are these voluntary groups that gather, read the Scripture, and try to discern God in their lives. So they become a learning and a support group of how to translate the gospel into everyday-ness. I was impressed with what a few of them had said. One man said, "I'm a born Catholic and have gone to church every Sunday, went to confession regularly, and that was it. Religion for me was very private. But since I've been in this sharing group, reading the gospel, and getting a kind of faith community, I find myself, now, at work, standing up and raising ethical questions. When decisions are being made, I find myself asking, 'Well, is this the right thing?' I find myself challenging decisions that I think are going to hurt people. I would never have done that before. And I expected to get blasted as trying to be holier than the pope, but I was amazed at how much appreciated that stance is. As if my co-workers were looking for something like that."

A woman says this: "I've been in my job maybe twenty-five, thirty years, and since I have been a part of this group where we do meet and share the gospel and support one another, the last two or three years I have found myself saying to my troubled co-employees, 'Do you want me to pray for you?' I have found myself inviting them, 'Would you like to share a prayer with me? I know that you're troubled.' " And again, she comes up with the same kind of recognition, that people, far from being put off, were very grateful. Because of the impact of the gospel, she and the man I spoke with were doing things they never would have done before, or said before, or witnessed to before, and they found people responsive.

So it seems to me when we talk about the generation of re-learning coming up, it is obvious that we need reteaching, and it is equally obvious that the teachers are in this building right now. People are hungry for God. People have a deep, innate thirst for God.

There's a well-known psychiatrist named Gerard May, who's just written a very fine book called *Addiction and Grace*, and I'd just like to repeat some of his words here. He says, "After twenty years of listening to the yearnings of people's hearts, I'm convinced that all human beings have an inborn desire of God. Whether they are consciously religious or not, this desire for God is our deepest longing and our most precious treasure. It gives us meaning. Some of them have repressed this desire, burying it beneath so many other interests that we are completely unaware of it. Or we may experience it in different ways—as a longing for wholeness, fulfillment, completion. Regardless of how we describe it, it is a longing for love. It is a hunger for love, to be loved, and to move closer to the source of love."

And then he adds: "But something gets in the way of our inborn desire of God. The longing at the center of our hearts repeatedly disappears from our awareness and its energy is usurped by forces that are not at all loving. Our desires are captured, and we give ourselves over to things, that in our deepest honesty, we really do not want."

And again, that's where you come in. It's not that you would have an unreceptive audience. It's not that you would preach a message foreign to human nature. When in your own quiet way you make ethical decisions; in your own quiet way, even if you lose some financial gain, you're honest; in your own quiet way you refuse to cheat, or be unfaithful; in your own quiet way you raise issues that deal with humanity; in your quiet way you become known as a witness to truth and decency, you are not going to jangle something foreign. You are going to jangle something that people want to say, but don't have the courage to say. You're going to resonate that deepest desire for God that they cannot name.

So this is what the gospel means. Unless you take up your cross daily; unless you make these daily decisions, some of which are easy, some of which are joyous, and some which cause pain; unless you do that, you're not worthy of Jesus. So taking up the cross doesn't mean running around looking how you might physically suffer, taking up the cross means how you can run around and call forth from people what's already in their hearts—the burning desire for God.

26

$\mathcal{P}eace$

Luke 10:1–12

I had something entirely different in mind prepared for you, but yesterday a priest friend of mine who belongs to a missionary order stopped in; and in the course of the time, he was anxious to share with me a little story.

And because this very brief story touches on one of the themes of the gospel, I thought that I would set aside my own thoughts for the moment and share with you the story he told me. It concerns one of the priests of their order, Father Tony Williams, who had been a missionary in Tanzania for about sixteen, seventeen years.

In the course of his time there, he had picked up abdominal cancer. He thought it was something minor until careful research showed that it was more widespread than they thought. When it became obvious that this was a serious thing, he finally went through the operation, and it seemed to have taken care of it, and in a comparatively short time, he was back on his feet and also back on his job.

Father Tony Williams was a very upbeat and ingratiating, very personable man. And one of those people, wherever he went, people loved him. He was gracious and kind; nice sense of humor.

He came back to the United States after his stint, and after a few years the cancer kicked up again, and to such a degree that, in fact, it was only a matter of time for him to live. In the time that he spent at the headquarters, the motherhouse, different ones would come and visit him and talk to him.

Well, one day he asked for the father general, the father superior, and he came to visit Father Tony, who told him, "I have something to tell you. As I've been lying here sick, I had an experience the other night that I would like to share."

He said, "I was lying here in my sickness, trying to pray and finding it very hard. I was gazing at the crucified head of Christ, and as I was gazing at it, trying to pray, suddenly the eyes seemed to grow luminous. And as the eyes grew luminous and looked at me, and I looked at them, suddenly, somehow, I felt myself drawn into the picture and I found myself on Calvary. And I arrived on Calvary precisely at that time and moment when Jesus was being crucified and the soldiers were hammering the nails into his hands."

He continued, "But you can imagine how utterly surprised and shocked I was when one of the soldiers' faces was mine! And I asked the Lord, 'Have I been that terrible? After all, I've led a comparatively good and decent life. I haven't really done anything that horrible. Is it possible that my sins are crucifying you? Are they that evil and bad?' " And he said Christ turned to him and looked at him, and with a gentle smile, said, " 'Tony, whatever they are, your sins are forgiven. My peace I give to you.' "

And then Tony said, "The face, my face, on that soldier disappeared, and I kind of came out of it. And ever since," he told the superior, "I have found this enormous peace, that peace that's in the gospel, that Jesus spoke about."

And so as the time drew near, he gathered his family. He came from a comparatively large family. I think he had five or six brothers and sisters; his parents were still living. And so they came and visited his sickroom as he sensed the time was near. He said goodbye to all of his brothers and sisters and nieces and nephews, and his mother and father. And you can imagine, many, many tears were shed.

But what struck everybody who went into the room—and they all said the same thing—was when you entered his room, you had this unspeakable sense of peace. It just emanated from the room, and emanated from him. "And when he spoke with us, as agitated and sad as we were, we seemed to drink in that peace."

Then Tony said, "I've only a few minutes left." He said, "I have one dying wish for you. My wish for you is the peace that I have received from knowing that Jesus not only died for my sins, but that he loves me with such an incredible love. At this point in my life I'm looking forward to seeing once more this Christ who loves me so much and who gives me such peace."

A few minutes later he closed his eyes and died. And he died with a big smile on his face. The priest was there who saw and witnessed all this and told me.

That true story says a great deal about this gospel reading. Jesus said, "When you go to any place, the first thing you say is 'Peace to this house—shalom.' The peace not as the world gives, but as I give it." And so maybe that's just the thought we want to take today.

Peace comes from knowing that you're loved by God. Peace comes from knowing that Jesus died for our sins. Peace comes from knowing that when all is said and done, that right relationship with Jesus is all that matters. Peace comes from the fact that when all of us have to let go, as we must, we do not fall into nothingness, but we fall into the arms of Christ. It's a peace that is incapable of being given by anything or anybody else in this world. Except Christ.

And as a sign of this we have the life and the death of this man Tony Williams, who was not remarkable in any way, particularly. His simple, quiet humor and his experience of peace that came from Christ—these are what he has left as a legacy to his family and his community. And a legacy that I share with you.

So Jesus says to us, his disciples, "When you leave this

building today, and you go into your work-a-day world, wherever you go, say 'Peace,' and by that you mean to imply to your friends, and your neighbors, and your co-workers, that 'I know a peace that only comes from Christ, and I'd like to share that with you.' "

"Your sins are forgiven. Go in peace."

27

Holy Thursday

John 13:1–17

To understand the episode that we are celebrating, the washing of the feet, we have to turn away from John's gospel and get the leading clue from St. Luke.

Luke says in Chapter 22: "As the disciples were on their way to this last supper, a dispute also arose among them as to which of them was the greatest." If you remember this argument you can understand what happened and what it caused.

You know, for example, that in the East, in Palestine, the roads are unpaved. They carry the debris of animals, the debris of the dust, the dirt, the desert. That is why at each household door there is a water pot and a servant to dry one's feet.

Because there was no servant in this apostolic group, the apostles used to take turns doing this duty. But as you can see, they got into such a state of competitive pride that no one took up the task. And so they all walked into the house, each one filled with his own isolated pride, and sat down with unwashed feet. And the feet remained unwashed and no one took up the task until Jesus did, much to their mortification.

And as always, what he did, he did for a twofold purpose. The first purpose, of course, was to teach his followers the way it should be with Christians. He said, as you recall, that among the pagans, those who exercise authority are those who lord it over others, who demand preferential treatment, who wait to be waited on. "But with you," he said "it must be different. Let him who would be greatest among you, serve. Let the one who would be the master, be the slave. You call me Lord and Master and indeed, you are right. And if I, Lord and Master, have washed your feet, this is an indication of what the Christian community should be identified as. A community that goes forth and washes the feet of the world."

When I washed the feet a few minutes ago, I tried to do, with great humility, what Jesus did. I refused to look up to see the faces that belonged to those feet, simply because when Jesus washed the feet, he didn't look up. And whether it was the feet of Peter, or the feet of John, or the feet of Judas Iscariot, he didn't want to know the difference. He just wanted everybody to know that his love went out to them all, regardless whether they were the scum of the earth or prince among princes.

He did not want to see whether the face was beautiful or ugly; whether the face had virtue or vice written on it; whether the face was noble with dignity or sodden with drink and drugs; whether the face was upon a virtuous body or one that had gone through every house and every indecency in town. He did not know, or want to know, whether the face was black or white or red or yellow; whether it belonged to a man or a woman; slave or free; master or servant; Jew or Gentile.

For his community of believers must do as he did. "This is my body given for all of you. This is my blood shed for all. And I wash humankind's feet of its grime in sin, its indignity. I will not look up to make preferences."

That was the first lesson. The apostles learned it well much to their shame. This is what it means. This is the summation of the gospel. This is the end product of three years of knowing Christ Jesus: to serve humankind, and if we would aspire to be the greatest, then we get on our knees and wash the feet of all manner of humankind.

There is a second lesson. It has to do with the eucharist. Jesus is saying this: "You want to know what we're doing at this last supper? By my taking bread and wine, this cup, and sharing it among you, by my washing of the feet, I want you to understand what the eucharist would mean. The eucharist would be forever a living symbol that I am in your midst urging you to do that service. When I take this bread and say, 'Look, this is my body, and it's broken for you. This is the cup of my blood shed for you.' And so the Christian community should do that as well."

Perhaps the greatest symbol of the washing of the feet is when Jesus took that chalice, that cup; and very likely he held it up for a moment so that they could get the full impact. And in effect he was saying, as he says now at every eucharist, "A cup is poured out"—like parents, who pour out their lives.

A cup is emptied, and so are we emptied of strength and health in sickness and old age. A cup is filled, and so are we when we come to heaven; or when we come to each new day with its happiness, with its new beginnings. A cup is held out, like life is held out and shared every day. The cup is broken, as life is broken by sin, and its continuity is broken by death. But God's love has the power to make it whole again. To share the cup at Mass means that we share life with all of its sorrows and joys strengthened by Jesus, who is still with us. The washing of the feet meant that too.

So this is the holiest night of the year, as it were, the time when we Christians harken back to almost 2000 years ago; into a room which was maybe about half the size of this building, with apostles gathered like yourselves, and your twelve represented here by these members of the community, from the youngest to the oldest, men and women, far and wide, of far different origins. And we have met in order to remember what the eucharist means.

Jesus, in our midst, urges us, "Take your body and give it for others, and break it for others, in love. Take the cup of your blood and pour it out and empty it, and hold it out and help restore others so that fractured humankind may be whole again. Whenever you eat this bread and drink this cup, you do it, truly, in memory of me."

My friends, as we now continue the eucharist on this most solemn night, let's try to put ourselves back into that cenacle. Let's pretend that we're there and Jesus has just washed our feet and we're ashamed, but now we have the message. And during the rest of this eucharist, as we come up to receive that broken bread and share that cup, we promise anew to Jesus to be his living community and his presence; and resolve that all shall know we are Christians by our love, one for the other.

28

+

Abraham and Sarah:
A Golden Jubilee

Genesis 18:1–10

I would like to reflect with you on that first reading. You heard that Abraham and Sarah, as typical nomads wandering the deserts of the Mid-East, were suddenly aware that three strangers had come their way, not knowing that the strangers were God and God's angels. And so very typically, they accosted the strangers and they pressed upon them hospitality.

You have to recognize that in the Mid-East, even to this day, hospitality is the hallmark of a very true and noble human being. This is equivalent to all the college degrees, or anything else, that we think a great deal of. To give hospitality was such a profound reality. It's difficult for us to understand how profound it was, because these were people living in very harsh times.

Food was extremely scarce and hard to come by. So, in effect, you see what the hospitality says: "When I take my food that keeps me alive, and I share it with you, I am thereby sharing something of my life, my very self." No wonder that hospitality was so meaningful. And even to this day, if you come upon some of the Bedouin tribes traveling through the desert, you cannot get by, as a stranger, unless you go and share a meal with them even though they deprive themselves. And so such hospitality, therefore, is a concern for others at a cost to self.

And as I was thinking on the Scripture of Abraham and Sarah, and their entertaining of the strangers, I also could not help but think that this is what marriage is fundamentally like. It is a hospitality of marriage. It is a concern for others at a cost to self.

We know too well what the inhospitality of marriage costs. The broken marriage; the physical, economic, social, emotional, and spiritual harm. And some of you have been through that pain of divorce and you know how it lasts with the children until they die. And that's a sad thing. But on the other hand, we know the hospitality of the marriages that have endured; and keep us from cynicism, and give us hope, and make a statement.

And all of this happens to fit in, because we are here not only to reflect upon Abraham and Sarah, but also to celebrate the fiftieth wedding anniversary of a couple in our community, Bill and Mildred Lanzaron, and to reflect upon the endurance of marriage in general. And when I think of this couple or any couple who have been together for many years, I think immediately of Abraham and Sarah, who lived together also a long time. And I think that fifty years together must mean that a couple has given a lot of hospitality to one another, hospitality to their children, hospitality to their friends, hospitality to the stranger, and to those in need.

I think that there is no human life that is ideal, and so any couple who have been together for many, many years have had their ups and downs. They have known death of family members, of course. They have known difficulties. They have known sickness and struggles with disease. So there is no ideal, trouble-free relationship. What is important is rather the fact that the hospitality has endured.

One of the enormous factors in most marriages that endure was a factor for Abraham and Sarah. They unknowingly entertained God—faith was an incredible part of their lives. Marriages that last have to endure through thick and thin, and the reality and centrality of God keeps the man and woman hospitable to their marriage and to one another.

There's an interesting thing, as you heard at the end of the Abraham and Sarah story, because after this gracious hospitality, the stranger, who is God, says to Abraham and Sarah, "You've been so good to me that this time next year I will come back, because Sarah, in her old age, will bear a child." Now what seems to be going on here is this: What God is really saying is that because of your hospitality of marriage, I will give you new life, represented by the child, Isaac.

And I think that is the promise that we celebrate when we gather to reflect on the endurance of a marriage—the promise of a newness of life that comes from the cost to each member of the couple, and the growing together as a couple. The new life that is theirs now and continues hereafter. I think that's probably what is meant here.

And woven into this promise of life is also, of course, a strong sense of reality. Fifty years of hospitality makes a couple real and genuine people, with few illusions, a great deal of hope, much love, incredible faith; and therefore, again, that makes them real.

I thought of what now is termed to be something of a cliché, but which nevertheless, is applicable here. When I was thinking of Abraham and Sarah, and when I was thinking of Bill and Mildred—this couple before us who have been married fifty years—my thoughts turned to the old Velveteen Rabbit episode. And although it's been read many times, I think we ought to listen to it with fresh ears because it's so applicable. It's that particular scene, you recollect, when the velveteen rabbit and the old skin horse are lying in the pantry, and the

young velveteen rabbit is starting to make conversation to
while away the time, and asks:

> "What is real? Does it mean having things that buzz in-
> side of you, and a stick-out handle?"
>
> "Real isn't how you are made," said the skin horse.
> "It's a thing that happens to you. When a child loves you
> for a long, long time, not just to play with, but really
> loves you, then you become real."
>
> "Does it hurt?" asked the rabbit.
>
> "Sometimes," said the old skin horse, for he was al-
> ways truthful. "But when you are real, you don't mind
> being hurt."
>
> "Does it happen all at once, like being wound up?" he
> asked, "or bit by bit?"
>
> "It doesn't happen all at once," said the old skin horse,
> "you become. It takes a long time. That's why it doesn't
> often happen to people who break easily, or have sharp
> edges, or have to be carefully kept. Generally by the time
> you are real, most of your hair has been loved off, your
> eyes drop out, you get loose in the joints, and very shab-
> by. But these things don't matter at all, because once you
> are real, you can't be ugly, except to people who don't
> understand."
>
> "I suppose you are real," said the rabbit, and then he
> wished he had not said it, for he thought the old skin
> horse might be sensitive. But the old skin horse only
> smiled.
>
> "The boy's uncle made me real," he said. "That was a
> great many years ago, but once you are real, you can't be-
> come unreal again. It lasts for always."

That's a part of the hospitality of marriage, isn't it? It makes
people real, and the nice thing is that it lasts for always.

29

+

A Wedding Homily
For Mai and John Cleary
John 6:60–68

It is interesting to note, when you listen to or read the Scriptures, how so very often Jesus asks a question. There are lots of them, such as the one in today's gospel.

I would like to share with Mai and John and the rest of you three questions that Jesus asked in different episodes in his life because I think they might be questions that might well fit this marriage that we're about to celebrate, or indeed any marriage.

The first question is: "Who do you say that I am?" Mai and John will ask that of each other many times. It might be rephrased differently, like, "What do you think I am?", but it's the same question. The answers will be different depending on their mood and the time of life that they're in.

"Who do you say that I am?" There are the negative answers, two examples of which we could draw from television comedians—Archie Bunker would reply, I suppose, with "Meathead," and Phyllis Diller made fun of her husband by calling him "Fang." Then there are the idealized responses. The young man and woman about to be married, walking along a lake, and in a bit of poetry, the young man looks at the ocean and cries, "Roll on, ocean, roll on." And she, looking starry-eyed into his eyes, says, "Oh Marvin, you're wonderful. It's rolling."

Then there are the realistic responses to this question, "Who do you say that I am?" Joanne Woodward gives a good, realistic response because she's been married to Paul Newman, for, what, twenty-five or thirty years? She says, "I find it difficult to understand why my husband is still such a great sex symbol for the teenagers. After all, he's fifty years old, he has six kids, and he snores." And maybe there, you see, there's an answer that's more realistic.

Who do you say that I am—and whom am I marrying? I'm marrying a very fallible human being. One who can reach great heights, and can reach the depths. But one whose identity gets unfolded as the years go by: from spouse to friend; to lover; to husband; to father; to mother. There'll be many identities and many responses. And if all goes well for Mai and John, as time goes on the answers get clearer, and finally you're able to answer like Peter, after three years of hanging around with Jesus. He says, "I can't say anything else. You are the messiah, the son of the living God."

And true love gives that answer. Finally and ultimately, when you go through the hateful answers and the indifferent answers and the idealized answers, true love comes up with something like that: "You are the one for me; my redeemer, my friend, without whom my life would simply be meaningless."

There's a second question that Jesus asks in the gospel. You might recall after he talked about giving his body and blood as food, and people said, "This is a bit much," he asked his own friends, Peter and the rest, when he saw some leaving, "Will you also go away?" And that's going to be a question that spouses will ask at different times in a marriage. "Will you also go away?" or the more direct "Why don't you get out of here?" "Go play in traffic!" Things like that.

And again, you see, it's going to be at that death-birth time that this question gets asked. The death-birth time is when you really get crunched and hurt, and it's at that moment that the seeds are sown. If you hang in there, something grander and more beautiful works through. Most divorces come in that period when the dying's going on. If they would just hold on a little bit longer to where there's a renewal of life. That's the period of time when a husband and wife that I know (who have been married, oh, twenty-five years or so and they're very good Catholics; they're very religious people, a fairly good union, the husband's a good provider, the wife's a good housekeeper; they go to church every Sunday; and they have the custom of saying their prayers together every night before they go to bed) did have one problem that seemed insurmountable. That problem was they they could not end up a conversation without an argument.

So finally the wife decided she'd had enough, but because of her religious convictions, divorce was out of the question. She had a better idea, however. One night as the couple settled down for their nightly prayer, she said to her husband, "Look, we simply have to put an end to this terrible situation; we can't go on like this anymore. Since this is the first day of Pentecost, why don't we make a novena that things will change? Let's pray that the Lord will call one of us home to him. Then I can go and live with my sister." That's a bit of a joke, of course, but the point is that in any marriage there are going to be times during which it is going to take all the humor, creativity, and endurance the couple can muster just to get through to the point of renewal.

"Will you also go away?" Right now the answer for Mai and John is "never." But realistically, the answer at times is going to be "I don't know." And they've got to hang in there because that's a life-death question that Jesus asked. And his friends had that moment of "should we leave or should we stick this out?", and they stuck it out to something grander. So I suggest for these two, and for all of us, that's a good question on marriage day.

The third question, of course, comes at the end, after the resurrection when Jesus is on the shore and they're cooking fish, and Peter, who had denied him three times, gets this third question, which you know: "Do you love me?"

Interestingly enough, that's the question in a famous duet. If you turn on your imagination, you're sitting in a theatre, here's the stage, and Mai and John—or rather Teyve and Golda—come in for their last duet. You recall *Fiddler on the Roof?* Here's the duet:

"Golda, do you love me?"

"Do I what?"

"Do you love me?"

"Do I love you? With our daughters getting married and this trouble in the town, you're upset. You're worn out. Go inside. Go lie down. Maybe it's indigestion."

"Golda, I'm asking you a question. Do you love me?"

"You're a fool."

"I know. But do you love me?"

"Do I love you? Twenty-five years I've washed your clothes, cooked your meals, cleaned your house, given you children, milked the cows. After twenty-five years, why talk about love right now?"

"Golda, the first time I met you was on our wedding day. I was scared."

" I was shy."

" I was nervous."

"So was I."

"But my father and mother said we'd learn to love each other. So I'm now asking, Golda, do you love me?"

"I'm your wife."

"I know, but do you love me?"

"Do I love him? For twenty-five years I've lived with him, fought with him, starved with him. Twenty-five years my bed is his. If that's not love, what is?"

"Then you do love me?"

"I suppose I do."

"And I suppose I love you, too."

And the two of them go up to the end of the stage, and hold hands, and they sing to the audience, "It doesn't change a thing, but even so, after twenty-five years, it's nice to know." And that's the answer to our third question for marriage: "Do you love me?"

And so I leave for Mai and John these three questions to weave in and out of their marriage: "Who do you say that I am?" "Will you also go away?" and "Do you love me?" And if they can remember the responses of Jesus' friends to these questions, and if they can remember that these questions are woven into every life, and if they will sweat through, work through, and pray through the responses, then some day twenty-five years, or let's say fifty years from now, old and aged and decrepit, Mrs. Cleary and Mr. Cleary will come to the world stage and they'll sing their duet, which is a way of bearing witness. And they'll ask each other in song, in their old age, "Do you love me?"

And they'll respond with life and death comments throughout all their years. And you know what their conclusion will be? After twenty-five or fifty years, "I suppose I do. It doesn't make much of a difference, except right now it's nice to know and nice to proclaim."

So that's our prayer for you. Ask the right questions, and give the right answers.

30

A Funeral Homily
For Sally Gassert
Luke 24:13–35

When St. Luke sat down to write this gospel story, it was not just a fancy and interesting telling of a post-resurrection tale. He was writing for his community, and like so many other communities, it had to face the question of death. And with death, the feeling of isolation and alienation and shattering distress.

And in the story Luke proposed a number of things for his parish congregation of his time and for our community, in our time. He's got wrapped up in there three elements as to how and why and where a community can find its own inner healing when faced with death, as the first one was faced with the death of its leader, Jesus Christ.

Notice the first element: Scripture. When these excited and distressed and grieving disciples were excitedly talking on the way to Emmaus, the stranger approached, and after their dialogue, what did he do when he got the news of their distress, anxiety, and hurt? He opened to the Scripture. And Luke is saying, in effect, in your grief, facing death, that's the first step to healing—open up the Scripture. And so we open them and as we cast our eye here and there, what is it we read? We read of Jesus standing there saying: "I am the resurrection and the life; he who believes in me shall never die." Or again, "The one who would save his life will lose it, but the one who loses his life for my sake shall find it." Or, "Just as the seed is planted in the ground, if it remains on the ground, it is sterile; but if it is planted deep, it springs up with fruitful blade. So shall I be planted in the earth and rise up again." And so shall you, by implication.

And again in Scripture, "Though your sins be as red as scarlet I will make them as white as snow." Or yet, in Jeremiah, "Behold, tell the people I have loved you with an everlasting love."

And so as we review all of these things we turn to Scripture and we see the basis of what we are celebrating today—the death of someone we have known and loved. And through the words of Scripture, we can celebrate in hope because Jesus is the resurrection and the life, and Sally believed in him. And all those who believe will be raised up on the last day.

And because of that we take our tears and our sorrow and we mingle them with hope and even with joy. And that's why, from the very beginning, Christians have always caught that double feeling about death: the very human tears at losing someone we have known and loved, and yet that very distinct undercurrent of joy.

And the church picks that up in its liturgy, and you notice, for example, that we have flowers that we usually associate with joyous times. And we are wearing the white vestments that we associate with weddings. And in the early church, if they had had newspapers, the headline for Sally Gassert would have been: "Sally Gassert Celebrated Her Birthday on the Day of Her Death." Because in the old days, they considered the day you died your birthday, when you were really born again, when, without encumbrance and without obliqueness, directly face to face, as Paul says, you would look on the vision and the face of the Father. And all because Scripture opened up to us the meaning of life and death in Jesus.

The second element that Luke gives for healing the community is one that Sally knew very well—and we know here. How did they recognize Jesus? They recognized Jesus in the breaking of the bread. And as people go through their anger, understandably, and as people are caught face to face with death—death of little children, innocent people, teenagers being killed instantly, the long pain of cancer for Sally—and as we scream and rant and rave and wrestle with these things, and get angry with God, we still find the answer, and Jesus, and healing in the breaking of the bread.

And we remember that when we celebrate our eucharist. Jesus said, "I'm going to take my body and make it food, so this bread can be broken and given; and my blood will be distributed for the forgiveness of sins." And all of us who approach death with our tale of folly and sin know Jesus has been broken for us; and the moment that we thought was doom and destruction and despair—lo and behold—we discovered him in the breaking of the bread.

And every time we in the Christian tradition here meet around the altar and celebrate the eucharist, we celebrate the life, death, and resurrection of Jesus, and our own life, death, and resurrection—and we discover his presence there. Sally, who received communion everyday from the hands of her relatives, knew what it meant, and how important that eucharist was—to discover Jesus.

The final element that Luke gives us is community. You notice at the end of that story, the first thing the disciples did when they got the good news and recognized Jesus, they went back to the community at Jerusalem. And here's the final point to healing: the community, the community of the church, the community of this parish, the community of one's family and friends. And it is only in this community that we exchange our hurts and exchange our pains, and exchange our faith, and exchange our hope, and exchange our love, and then healing takes place.

We look around this community gathered here, and we know some of you from this parish have tasted death—some of you have lost little children; some of you have lost your spouse; many of you have lost your parents. And you and I who have been through these things, we're gathered here to share with one another, and to heal one another by our presence, by our scars, and by our faith.

It is in this community that we find renewed meaning. It is in this community that we find a wider family than our biological family. It is in this community of faith that we are restored, and eventually you know what happens. It's what happens to some of you. We become "wounded healers" ourselves. So deeply wounded by death and hurt and pain and sickness, we get that grace-filled power that, next year this time, when someone else faces death, we have the words to say, and the heart to give, and the healing to offer because, like Jesus, we've got five wounds in our heart and our bodies, and we're able to touch each other in a dimension we were not able to do before, when we had not known pain and death. And the community makes that possible.

The community, like the family, also accepts us as we are: our good and our bad, our cleverness and our stupidity. And so Luke has revealed to us in this gospel a scenario for what we are about today. We will be healed through Sally's death, through Scripture, through the eucharist, and through community.

Sometimes at funerals we don't talk much about or praise the person who had died, and that is because the funerals, in a sense, are for our benefit—for the living—because you and I have yet to undergo this experience, and someone's death prepares us for it. And whether we are a Catholic, Protestant, Jew, or atheist, none of us can fail to be moved at this.

Sally was prepared more than usual by Scripture, because every day she read it. She kept her wits about her, her intelligence and her humor. A couple of days before she died, at a time when some thought she might be very close to death, I went over to see her and I read Scripture. She had a favorite passage from Ecclesiastes, and one of the other people there got up and read that. Even in her sickness she said, "That was lovely, but it was the wrong reading." And I was there the next day to anoint her with the sacrament of the sick, and we had a long private talk together—very fruitful and very beautiful. Some of the things I can share—not many. But she said, "Do you think—you know—what does it feel like to die?" I said, "Sally, I've never been through it; I don't know. The only thing I can tell you is what I read about Oscar Wilde. When he was dying, on his death bed, he opened his eyes and looked around and said to the people gathered around the bed, 'Well, if this is dying, I don't think much of it.' "

She smiled at that because Sally was a literary buff. She said, "Do you think I'm dying?" I said, "Sally, I don't know; I think you probably are. Yet on the other hand, I've seen people suddenly get cured and get better, too. However," I said, "knowing you, you're a very private person, like myself, and probably if you had the choice, if you got well and you were—next week—walking around in full health, you'd be a living miracle. And people would be coming up, touching the hem of your garment, and you'd get all kinds of publicity." I said, "Knowing you, you'd probably rather die." And she said, "Yes, I would."

I came over to give her Flannery O'Connor's letters, *The Habit of Being.* She already had it, much to my delight, because I wanted to give the book to someone else, really; and I told her that. Flannery O'Connor, as many of you know, was a Catholic writer who was ill and died of her sickness—and like Sally had to use a walker and two of those aluminum canes when she got around (she and Sally were very much alike). And there was one passage from one of her letters that I wanted to read to Sally, and so I said, "Sally, she's just like you. She's a great letter writer, this Flannery O'Connor. She's writing to a friend and she says, 'I decided I must be a pretty pathetic sight with these crutches. I was in Atlanta the other day at Davidson's Department Store. An old lady got on the elevator behind me, and as soon as I turned around, she fixed me with a moist, gleaming eye and said in a loud voice, "Bless you, darling." I felt exactly like the misfit in one of my stories. And I gave her a weakly lethal look. Whereupon, greatly encouraged, she grabbed my arm and whispered very loudly in my ear, "Remember what they said to John at the gate, darling." It was not my floor, but I got off. And I suppose the old lady was astonished at how quickly I could get away on crutches. I have a one-legged friend and I asked her what they said to John at the gate. She said she reckoned they said, "The lame shall enter first." This may be because the lame will be able to knock everybody else aside with their crutches.'" That's Sally—and I have no doubt that where she is is with the Lord God—and heaven help anybody in her way.

She had enough wit and intelligence right to the end. The day before she died, when I was visiting her, she said, "Did you get the book I sent over, *The View in Winter*"? And I said, "Yes; I didn't get to read it. It sounds great, a lovely nature book." She said, "No, no, it's not a nature book about winter. It's the story about people in the winter of their lives. It's a story of interviews with old people. There are lovely passages there and I have one for you." And I didn't know that, so last night I found the book. And sure enough, unlike Sally, who had a great respect for books, she had marked in a light pencil, a passage for me to read on page 239, I suspected, after she died. And it's a passage spoken by an old man about eighty-three. But apparently this must have expressed her thoughts somewhat since she took the trouble to mark it for me.

And here is an old, old man speaking: "If I find no home any longer in this world, it is because God has been withdrawing me, my love, my treasures, my remembrances, my hopes, from a place where the frost-wind of death touched every precious thing, where no good can last; but night falls, and only icy solitude and silence remain. This is no home, this is but a lodging." This old man, by the way, was also completely deaf, and all of his senses were leaving him when he said this: "God is making all things dark and silent around me....I must begin to long for home. I seem almost asleep, but my heart is awake...memories sleep, thoughts sleep, but love is awake. It does not think or plan or labor to remember, but it loves. It is withdrawn from the surface of my life to the center....My God,

I would not die as the unconscious things—the frozen sparrow under the hedge, the dead leaf whirled away before the night wind."

I think Sally meant that very personally and God heard her prayer. She did not die as the unconscious things, and she did not die as the frozen sparrow under the hedge; or the dead leaves whirled away before the night wind. She died with consciousness, with readiness. She was so much at peace, as the family knows, after she received the sacrament of the sick, and had talked and recognized what was going on. She had made her peace with God, made her peace with the doctor, made her peace with herself. And so she had her community. And I couldn't help but think how again at the end of her life, as at the beginning, Scripture and eucharist and community were there.

And on the day of her burial they're here again, aren't they? Scripture has been read and rests on her coffin. The eucharist is celebrated, and community—here you are.

And lo and behold, by the grace of God, Sally has gone up where she began, in front of that baptismal font where she was first made a part of the community, and she ends her days there. She has not died as the frozen sparrow, she has died as a child of God. I think in these words, she recognized herself. And as her faculties were taken away one by one—her ability to walk, her ability to do things—she was being stripped of all the extraneous so she could get at the center—as this old man said.

I firmly believe that in the last hours of Sally Gassert's life, she had found the center, and having found the center, it was time to go home.

Lectionary References

12 Under the Broom Tree	1 Kings 19:1–9, Cycle B, 19th Sunday of the Year
13 Shadows: Father's Day	Luke 7:36–50, Weekday 1 & 2, Tuesday of the 24th Week of the Year
14 What Are We To Do?	Luke 3:1–19, Cycle C, 3rd Sunday of Advent
15 Designer Worth	Matthew 6:25–34, Cycle A, 8th Sunday of the Year
16 Radical Saints	Matthew 19:16–22, Weekday 1 & 2, Monday of the 20th Week of the year.
17 Halloween	Revelation 7:9–17, Cycle C, 4th Sunday of Easter
18 The Cross That Shapes Us	Mark 5:25–34, Cycle B, 13th Sunday of the Year
19 No More Wine	John 2:1–11, Cycle C, 2nd Sunday of the Year
20 Freeing the Voice	Mark 7:31–38, Cycle B, 23rd Sunday of the Year
21 All Saints	Revelation 7:1–8, Cycle C, 4th Sunday of Easter
22 The Good Woman	Luke 18:20–22
23 Companions	1 Kings, 19:1–9, Cycle B, 19th Sunday of the Year
24 Making Wishes Come True	Luke 4:14–19, Cycle C, 3rd Sunday of the Year